STEPHEN

Letters FROM Arabia

novum pro

© 2024 novum publishing

ISBN 978-3-99146-879-0
Editing: Charlotte Middleton
Cover photo: Stephen Bennett
Cover design, layout & typesetting: novum publishing
Internal illustrations: Stephen Bennett

The images provided by the author have been printed in the highest possible quality.

www.novum-publishing.co.uk

All rights of distribution, including via film, radio, and television, photomechanical reproduction, audio storage media, electronic data storage media, and the reprinting of portions of text, are reserved.

Printed in the European Union on environmentally friendly, chlorine- and acid-free paper.

For Annie

INTRODUCTION

اَلعربية   al-arabiya

The Arabic Language

I lived in Egypt and Jordan as a child, was witness to the first Palestinian uprising and sat on King Hussein of Jordan's knee. I came early to love the rugged beauty of the terrain and the courtesy of its people, feelings which were nurtured during brief encounters in my Royal Naval career in the early seventies and mid-eighties and reinforced during an extended period between two Gulf Wars working for admirals, three British and one an Arab Prince whom I later served as a civilian. This book aims to provide a flavour of a land and people that I came to love – a land of cardamom-flavoured coffee and camel trains, frankincense and fanatics, pirates and pearl fishers, a land where slights are sometimes forgiven but never forgotten and where friendships last forever.

Arabic is spoken in various dialects and variations throughout the Arabian Peninsula and its close neighbours and much more widely by the Islamic world in general. It is the language of the Holy Quran. Many of its words have entered our own language, such as 'admiral' (*amir al-bahr* – 'prince of the sea') whereas others we think of as Arabic, such as 'oasis', come from other languages, in that case Greek. To confuse matters further, 'Arabic' numerals (1, 2, 3, etc.) come originally from India, and numerals used in Arabia today are Persian (see Chapter 27).

Each chapter in this book uses one word from the Arabic twenty-eight-letter alphabet to adumbrate the fascinating world of Arabia as I experienced it in different guises. In Chapter 24, for example, we see that the word 'minaret' comes from the Arabic name for a lighthouse (*min'ara*) – a place of fire. But before we embark on this journey through the Arabic world, a few words about its script might be helpful.

Arabic script, which is written right to left with no capitals, comprises twenty-eight letters, one special sign and a few supplementary characters. Many Arabic words include a glottal stop. This is indicated by an apostrophe in the transliterated words shown in italic in these pages. Unlike English, it is strictly phonetic. Its alphabet includes some sounds unfamiliar to Western ears, for example the big aspirated 'HA' of the sixth letter *ḥaa'* (as in *baḥr* – sea) unlike the softer sound of its cousin, the twenty-sixth letter, also confusingly called *haa'*.

Each of the twenty-eight letters is written in three forms depending on whether it comes at the start or end of a word or between the two. Although it is cursive, i.e. 'joined up', there are six letters which cannot be joined to a letter which follows. An example is in the word for 'ministry' – *wizaara* – وزارة, in which neither (reading right to left) the *waaw, zaa', 'alif, raa'* nor *taa' maboota* (a supplementary character used at the end of many Arabic words) can be joined to those which follow.

There is no indefinite article in Arabic, but all nouns and associated adjectives (which come after the noun) are preceded by the definitive article *'al* or *'l* (joined to the noun in transliteration by a hyphen). So the Red Sea in Arabic would be *'al-baḥr 'l-'aḥmar* (the sea the red). If a definitive article proceeds words beginning with the fourteen so-called 'sun letters', the 'al' sound glides beautifully into the letter which follows it. So sun – الشمس – *al-shams* – is pronounced *ash-shams*. This gives Arabic, for all its guttural sounds, a mellifluous quality.

Arabic words are formed from the three-letter stem, the radicals, which maintain their order in the word. For example the three radicals *ḥaa', raa'* and *meem* can be found in the very similar words *ḥarem* (sanctuary – a sacred inviable space) and *ḥaram* (forbidden). The opposite of haram is *ḥalal* (lawful), not to be confused with *halaal* (new moon), which starts with the softer *haa'* letter.

There is no 'p – pee' or 'v – vee' in Arabic, so 'Pepsi' becomes 'Bebsi' and 'very' becomes 'ferry'. My first name, Steve, caused some confusion initially and my surname sounded like the Arabic for 'girl'. So to avoid being called 'stiff bint', I modified its pronunciation thereafter to Stef'n Beneet!

Some of the information I have encountered in preparing this book is conflicting, but therein lies the delight of jigsaw puzzles. I hope that my betters will point out glaring errors and turn up the missing pieces.

CONTENTS PAGE

Chapter	Letter				Chapter Title	
1	ا	'alif	أعراب	'aa'raab	Bedouin	13
2	ب	baa'	بحر	bahr	Sea	22
3	ت	taa'	تاريخ	t'areekh	History	29
4	ث	thaa'	ثور	thoor	Bull	37
5	ج	jeem	جمل	jamal	Camel	43
6	ح	haa'	حرب	harb	War	49
7	خ	khaa'	خيمة	khayma	Tent	55
8	د	daal	دشداشة	dishdasha	Robe	62
9	ذ	dhaal	ذهب	dhahab	Gold	67
10	ر	raa'	رأس	raas	Head	73
11	ز	zaa'	زوجة	zawja	Wife	80
12	س	seen	سفينة	safeena	Ship	86
13	ش	sheen	شمال	shamaal	North Wind	94
14	ص	saad	صدف	sadaf	Shell	102
15	ض	daad	ضابط	daabit	Officer	109
16	ط	taa'	طريق	tareeq	Trail	116
17	ظ	dhaa'	ظهر	dh'hr	Noon	124
18	ع	ayn	عبد	a'bd	Slave	130
19	غ	ghayn	غرب	gharb	West	136
20	ف	faa'	فلوس	faloos	Money	143
21	ق	qaaf	قبيلة	qabila	Tribe	149
22	ك	kaaf	كتاب	kitab	Book	155
23	ل	laam	لبان	labaan	Frankincense	161
24	م	meem	منارة	min'ara	Lighthouse	166
25	ن	noon	نجم	najm	Star	174
26	ه	haa'	هلال	halaal	New Moon	181
27	و	waaw	واحد	waahid	One	186
28	ي	yaa'	يسار	yas'ar	Left	191

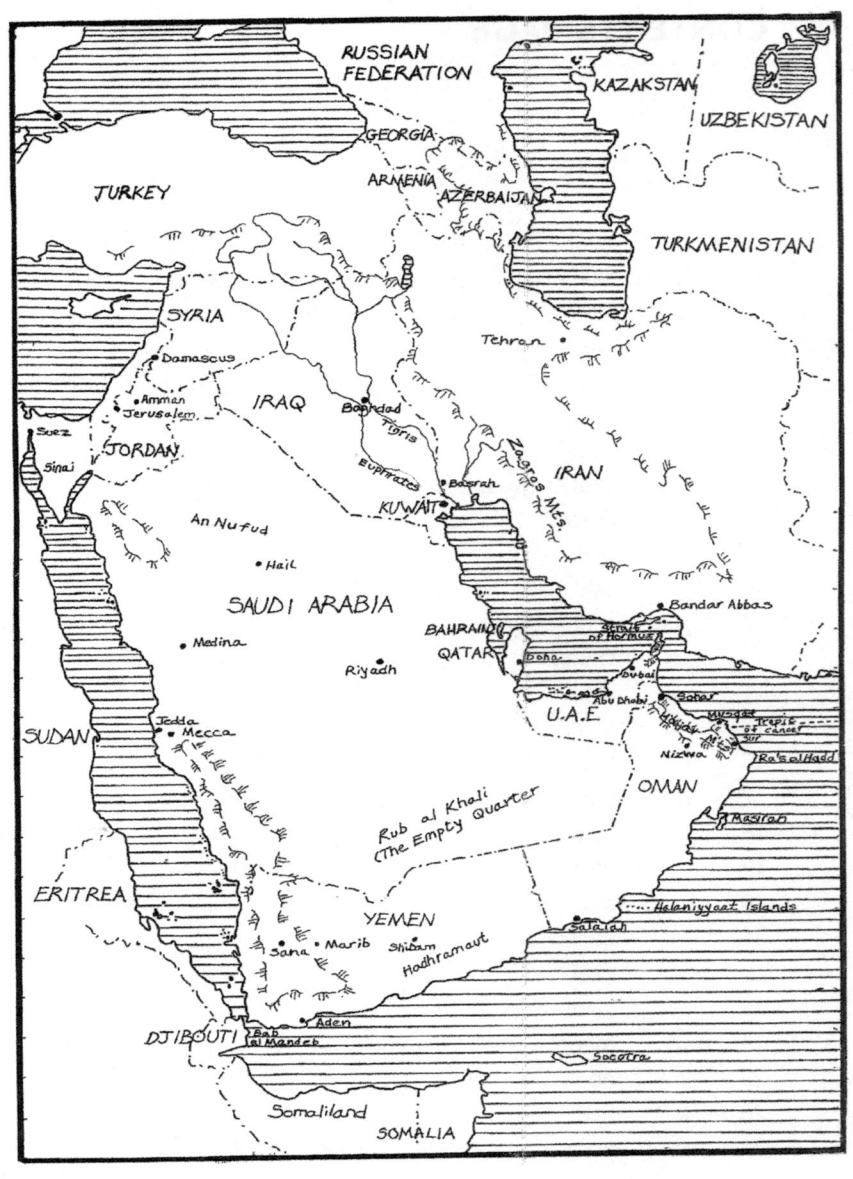

'The Rough Parallelogram' of Arabia (land borders are approximate)

CHAPTER 1

| ا | 'alif |
| أعراب | 'aa'raab |

Bedouin

My father, Lieutenant Colonel John Bennett MBE Royal Engineers, was posted to the Arab Legion in 1955. His boss, the commander of the Arab Legion since 1939 and King Hussein's miliary advisor, was Lieutenant General Sir John Bagot Glubb (Glubb Pasha as he was known – Pasha being the title accorded to miliary leaders in the Ottoman Empire[1]). My father never liked Glubb much, rather overbearing and stiff, he thought. King Hussein shared this view, and Glubb was asked to leave the following year but not before my father had supervised the construction of the lowest bridge in the world, four hundred metres below sea level, across the River Jordan. When he went to brief King Hussein, I was scooped up by the King to sit on the royal knee. I was six. This was my second introduction to the Arab world, having lived in the Canal Zone with my sister and twin brother, Andrew, since late 1950.

---

[1] Glubb's biography by General James Lunt is superbly told. Details of the bibliography for this book can be found at the back.

The Author with his twin brother and sister in Jordan 1956

It might have been my last introduction had not a burly army 'Sapper' intervened to prevent Andy from dragging me into the Red Sea at *al-'Ain al-Sokhna*, fifty-five kilometres south of Suez, a place I would return to thirty-three years later as a Royal Naval Lieutenant Commander during OPERATION HARLING (Chapter 15). I understandably became fascinated by the peoples who lived and had lived in this 'rough parallelogram' of land (as T. E. Lawrence described it) almost as large as India, the centre of *ish-sharq al-awsat* (*sharq* – East; *wast* – middle) – The Middle East.

C. M. Doughty, in his lyrical *Arabia Deserta*, said of it, 'Here is a dead land, whence, if a man die not, he shall bring home nothing but a perpetual weariness in his bones.' I could not disagree more. I brought home silver daggers unearthed from the deep recesses of the *is-suq* (market) in the desert border town of Sinaw in Oman, and pots hot from the kilns at Bahla, the ancient capital of Oman, dominated by a huge citadel protected by a crumbling twelve-kilometre-long wall. The character of those who have occupied this land is not always easy to emulate or quantify. The same person who pushes past you in a queue for free food will, when returning, suddenly recognise you, seize you by the hand and, smiling broadly, lead you to share his feast. It is this complex and contrasting character which we examine in this chapter.

South of the Fertile Crescent down the western and southern sides of the peninsula, from Syria (which the early Arabs called *sham*) to the Hadhramaut in Eastern Yemen, ran a series of well-watered mountainous regions which were able to support considerable populations. Because of its fertile nature, the Romans called it 'Arabia Felix' – the fortunate land. Pliny thought it fortunate because it was the source of 'the heaps of odours (frankincense) that are piled up in honour of the dead.' (See Chapter 23.) But it was regular rainfall, rather than frankincense, which made this the Lucky Land. Rain falling for centuries on the western limestone mountains drained northwards and eastwards to disappear into the desolate wastes to recharge vast subterranean aquifers of fossil water, thousands of years old.

Towards the rising sun lay great expanses of waterless desert including the vast sands of *ar-rubh' al-khali* – the Empty Quarter – wherein lay the fabled *'ubar* – the so-called 'Atlantis of the Sands'. The Empty Quarter's tamarisk-bush fringe fluctuates with unpredictable rainfall, but its heart is virtually waterless and totally silent, one of the few places on earth where no birds sing. The Empty Quarter (Arabs simply call it *ar-rimal* – the Sands) was crossed by Bertram Thomas and John Philby in the early 1930s and most famously by Wilfred Thesiger in the three years before I was born. His eyes still twinkled at the memory of those journeys when I lunched with him in Dubai in the late nineties.

Yemn means 'good luck, prosperity' in Arabic. The concept of auspicious good fortune and happiness in Arabic is always associated with the right-hand side (Chapter 28), the left (*yassar*) side with being small and easy. The Arabs, for whom the rising sun in the east was their reference point, not the European Pole Star, named the lucky well-watered land on their right-hand side *yameen*, hence Yemen.

From the fifteenth century BCE onwards, the population of Yemen grew steadily, and weaker tribes were forced eastwards towards the edge of the desert, where settled agriculture became impossible. Progressively they were pushed into the desert itself, where hardy tribes developed a precarious living breeding goats and camels. They became nomadic, exploiting what scarce resources there were. The al-'aa'raab[2], or Bedouin (plural of the Arab *bedu*), were born. In time their tribes gained control over 6.5 million hectares of grazing territories (*d'ar*) and their wells (*biir*), which they guarded fiercely, as anyone who has seen David Lean's *Lawrence of Arabia* will be able to testify. Before oil revenues made them less significant, tribal *d'ar* would contract, expand or move depending on the availability of ground water or grass generated from sporadic and unpredictable rain patterns and by the necessity to escape from rival stronger and greedier tribes. Insults by such tribes could not be tolerated and were avenged by vendetta. If a tribal member was murdered by another tribe, then any member of the offending tribe had to die in compensation. This non-specific eye-for-an-eye retribution gained acceptance in a world without any form of political law enforcement.

In very dry years, tribes were forced to move into the *d'ar* of friendly neighbouring tribes, which led to an overlap in grazing areas. To minimise conflict over this essential resource, tribes were bound together in loose confederations (*suff*). The fact that a tribe might be in more than one confederation added a cohesive structure to *bedu* life known as '*asabiyya*', or 'group spirit'. This allowed a tribe to cross the *d'ar* of other tribes in the same confederation when necessary, for example during the annual journey to local trading centres, where herded animals were exchanged for cooking utensils, weapons and those other

---

[2] The second letter of that name is the hard-to-pronounce ayn, which has no real equivalent in English, as the sound is made at the back of the throat like a guttural 'agh'.

commodities which the desert could not supply. What property there was and responsibility for its protection belonged to the male members of the tribe and was bequeathed from father to eldest son.

At the heart of this territory, so Lawrence wrote, was an archipelago of watered and populous oases called Kasim and Aridh, 'where lay the true centre of Arabia, the preserve of its native spirit, and its most conscious individuality. The desert lapped round and kept it pure of contact.' 'Oasis' and 'Bedouin' are English words. Arabs name the former *waha*. Herdsmen and warriors speak of themselves as either *badu* or *al-'aa'raab* – the inhabitants of the wastelands (*badia*). They do not consider settled Arabs as being in their class, referring to them witheringly as *fellahin* (peasants or farmers) or *ha*d*ari* (urbanites). The 'settled ones', those who created and tended the gardens and terraces, the irrigation systems and the water cisterns, were considered to be inferior – a resource to be exploited. The *wali* (local governor) of Salalah told Wilfred Thesiger in 1945 not to trust the settled men from the mountains – 'They are treacherous and thievish; altogether without honour.' One of my heroes, Captain Haines, Indian Navy, noted in the mid-nineteenth century that town-bred Arabs were 'timorous, indolent and much addicted to the use of tobacco'. By contrast, the Byzantine people found their *bedu* neighbours a significant irritation and were said to have imported, then loosed, lions from Africa to harry them!

The *bedu* lived by an ethical code – *muruwah* – which embodied not only a concept of manliness (courage, patience and fortitude) but a disregard of material wealth. Lawrence noted that 'only by having nothing can luxury be enjoyed, and long may it remain, however if luxury is taken away, what of it!' Glubb cautioned that although the Arab was regarded as being fickle, turbulent and insubordinate, he 'possesses another quality more rarely appreciated – that of total loyalty to a respected leader, a shaykh figure, whose hand they had shaken and whose word was law.'

In the Arabic mind, peace and the exercise of justice are inextricably linked. The three radicals which form the verb *salaha* – to make peace with – are the same which convey the sense of being good, virtuous, competent and trustworthy, not to be confused with *salaam* – peace, as in *as-salaamu alaykum* – peace be upon you, the universal greeting throughout Arabia. Every meeting, even though not the first of the day, starts with a handshake. One observer noticed that when shaking hands with a *bedu*, he did not make contact with the 'horny calloused palm' of a labourer but 'skin as soft as silk'. It is also the case that the longer the handshake, the more one has found favour.

Fourteenth-century Arab historian Ibn Khaldun in his *Muqaddima* wrote of the *bedu* that 'fortitude has become a character quality of theirs, and courage their nature. Because of their savagery they are the least willing of nations to subordinate themselves to each other, as they are rude, proud, ambitious and eager to be leaders, their individual aspirations rarely coincide.' They consider themselves to be manly (*muruah*) and elegant in manner (*zarf*) and proud that they were tempered in the fire of the desert, whose ways Lawrence wrote, 'were hard even for those brought up in them', but, according to him, whose 'cruel land can cast a spell which no temperate clime can match.' The poorest of them, whom Doughty called 'light-bodied, black-skinned and hungry-looking wretches' had all the arrogance of the aristocrat, calling themselves *'aseel* – of noble origin; thoroughbred. Another observer noted that the impoverished *bedu* 'gentleman of leisure' lived entirely in the present, unconcerned about the future. 'When time is not a dimension, it is a state of mind'. Thesiger, one of those Europeans who understood *bedu* mentality perfectly wrote, 'Their life is at all times desperately hard, and they are merciless critics of those who fall short in patience, good humour, generosity, loyalty or courage.' He saw that for them 'the danger lay not in the hardship of their lives, but the boredom and frustration they would feel when they renounced it'.

The *bedu* lived exclusively in black camel- or goat-hair tents (*bayt ash-sha'ar* – house of hair), raised camels or goats as their only livestock, conducted no manual labour and married only amongst themselves. They loved epic one-hundred-line poetry, mostly, so Glubb tells us, dealing with war, glory, women and wine. These were recited by tribal bards (*rawi*) or remembrancers, and the collection of poems which recounted tribal history came to be known as the *diwan* of a tribe, a word which subsequently came to mean a place of meeting and discussion, fitted with cushions or long seats – the derivation of our word 'divan'.

Within their camps, they were, and are, great boasters and terrific snobs. Thesiger noted that whoever lives with the bedu 'must accept *bedu* conventions and conform to *bedu* standards.' They 'argued endlessly, shouting in loud voices' and 'being garrulous by nature ... reminisce endlessly.' It has been my experience that while a dignified calm is maintained during discussions of technical matters, these outwardly tranquil men dissolve into arguments or gales of raucous laughter when matters become personal, such as the division of spoils, perceptions of injustice, matters of minor protocol or dress code, or the relative beauty of a camel, racehorse or 4WD (four-wheel drive vehicle). Use of the latter is not always as careful as it might be, however, as any observer of a road traffic accident in Arabia can vouch for. Crowds will converge on the damaged vehicle, not from any sense of mawkish curiosity but to be the first to remove the occupants and, heedless of blood on brand-new upholstery, drive the injured to hospital. This strict sense of chivalry has always existed. When the more moderate Crusaders encountered this code, they exported it back to Europe, where unlike in most of Arabia, it has in my experience withered considerably.

The majority of modern Arabs are very happy to discuss cultural differences. While courteously-delivered criticism from a trusted Western friend might be tolerated, a patronising or bullying attitude, or a show of impatience or anger, will lose its perpetrator any advantage previously gained. The easiest way to upset an Arab is to give any indication that his way of life is in any way inferior to Western practices. Other habits guaranteed to upset Arab hosts are a lack of effort to understand basic

Arabic language, using the left hand to eat with, failure to remove shoes when entering a private house or an admiration of an Arab's private belongings and showing the soles of one's feet or shoes. The Arabs, a race which, according to Lawrence, 'notice everything and forget nothing', are likely to take offence at over-familiarity, immoderate dress or behaviour or any slight, whether intentional or not. The recipient, whose naturally courteous nature will disguise his true feelings, may not indicate that he has been slighted, but the slight will never be forgotten.

This complex, contradictory and timeless character is epitomised by two examples, the first from the mid-eighth century CE when eighty sheikhs of the rival Umayyad dynasty were invited to dine with an Abbasid general. After being welcomed, they were slaughtered where they sat! The second example (quoted in James Lunt's biography of Glubb Pasha) is from the time just before the Arabian tribes rose in revolt against their Turkish masters. One of the *shereef* of Mecca's sons, Feisal, was sent to review troops accompanied by the Turkish Generalissimo and his delegation. When the Arab chiefs came up to be presented, one whispered, 'My Lord, shall we kill [the Turks] now?' .

Feisal replied 'No, they are our guests'!

The *bedu* revered their domesticated companions, those destructive agents of desertification, the camel and the goat. The former provided milk and carried the desert raiders to less well-defended settlements on the desert perimeter. Sir Alex Kirkbride, Resident in Transjordan, noted that raiding was like gambling: 'Like most variations of that amusement, it hardly ever enriched anyone and was a habit which people found most difficult to give up!'

These raids had other consequences. Unmaintained settlements crumbled as their 'settled' inhabitants retreated to better-defended towns. Over the rubble came inquisitive goats to uproot grass and shred the bark from trunks and branches. The *bedu* moved on, leaving destabilised gardens and fatally damaged trees. The unchecked wind scattered the topsoil and drove in the sand. This constant battle between the desert and the sown has continued for millennia. When the oil has gone, fingers of sand will reclaim the four-lane 'blacktop' highways. The settled will retreat to their towns and oases. The *bedu* will repopulate the desert. It has always been so.

CHAPTER 2

ب   baa'
بحر   bahr

Sea

The restricted waters of the Strait (not Straits!) of Hormuz make the comparatively shallow Persian/Arabian Gulf (The Gulf) one of the hottest and saltiest seas on earth. It loses more water through evaporation than it gains from rain and wadi water flowing into it. The balance is sustained by deep, powerful tidal flows funnelling in from the Gulf of Oman in which are suspended annual blooms of orange plankton – Red Tide. The anti-clockwise flow round the Gulf eventually piles up in the western fiords and inlets (*khawr*) of the indented and island-fringed Musandam Peninsula, the northern extremity in Oman of the *jebel al-hajar* (Rocky Mountain) range. The word 'Musandam' is derived from the ancient Roman name for Eastern Arabia – Mazoon. Ptolemy called Cape Mazoon *Asabon Promontorium*. We call it Ra's Musandam. A narrow arc of crumbling limestone, the Sibi Isthmus, tethers the peninsula to the mainland. It seems almost too insubstantial for the purpose, particularly as Mean Sea Level is some half a metre higher on the Gulf side than the other.

    There have been a number of schemes, some of them hairbrained, to cut through the isthmus or to insert a huge lock and join the two bodies of water on either side of it together, but common sense has so far prevailed. This region is home to countless seabirds and perhaps a few black leopards. It is also home to the equally exotic *ash-shibuh* or *kumzarah* tribe, who speak a complex dialect of negatives, a mixture of Arabic, Farsi and European, in which the imperative 'open' the door means 'shut it'. I sat with a *shibuh* shaykh once to try and dissuade him from servicing the outboard motors of the skiffs which plied the contraband cigarette trade across the strait to Iran, but his demeanour indicted clearly that I should 'shut it' too!

On the eastern side of the isthmus lies the deep, sheltered and astonishingly beautiful fiord of *khawr al-habalayn*. On the other, *khawr khasaibi* opens into the supposed pirate lair of *khawr ash-shams* (the inlet of the sun). This was named the Elphinstone Inlet by British hydrographic specialists sent to survey it in the nineteenth century to determine its suitability as a station on the Britain-to-India telegraph line. A century and a half later, another and far less experienced naval surveyor, Sub-Lieutenant Bennett, shaped the course of *HMS Beagle* towards an island (*jazira*) which lies just off it to the north-east. 'Peninsula' is *shiba jazirah* (almost an island), hence the name of the Al Jazirah TV news channel based on the Qatar Peninsula.

Viewed from the south, the cliffs of *jazirat musandam* resemble closely the head of a vast sleeping lion, giving the passage its name – *fakk al-assad* – the Lion's Jaw. Through these jaws run ferocious tidal flows generated by that half-metre drop in sea level. It is said that early mariners feared the passage and sent model boats ahead of them laden with sweets to propitiate the spirits (*jinn*) which spooked the sea into steep-sided waves and overfalls. The spirits were kind. *Beagle* sailed through the channel and rounded the long finger of *raas shuraytah* (*raas* – head) into the sheltered waters of *khawr al-quwayy*, later the home of the Royal Navy of Oman's naval base *jazirat umm al-ghanam*, or Goat Island. With the late afternoon sun lifting a curtain of shadows over the limestone cliffs, *Beagle*'s anchor rattled down, sending rust flakes and cormorants flying. Next morning at dawn, a party of eight led by my mentor, Commander Richard Campbell, twenty years later my captain during the Falklands War, started the long, hot climb to the summit of *jebel shams*, the peak which dominates the peninsula. The task in those pre-satellite navigation days was to conduct geodetic observations, just as our predecessors had one hundred and fifty years earlier. A similar peak in the south of Oman, *jebel kinkeri*, was climbed in

1835 by Lieutenant Jardine, Indian Navy, 'an officer whom no trifling difficulties could deter from accomplishing the wishes of his superior' (Captain Haines). He managed the extremely difficult ascent with his theodolite strapped to his back 'only by great perseverance'. I know how he felt!

We reached the peak at noon, and looking westwards, my binoculars tracked a huge pod of dolphins rippling down the coast towards a region known since antiquity as *as-sirr*. This coastal strip tapers as it meets the western side of the *al-hajar* mountains, and at its northern end lies a creek which has long been used as a refuge and rallying point for Arabs and their invaders. The Persians called the region, in what is now the UAE, Julfara and its capital Julfar. Since the expulsion of the Persian garrison in 1744, it has been known as Ra's al-Khaimah. The low-lying south-eastern coastal area from Ra's al-Khaimah ancient Dilmun was known to the Arabs as *al-bahrayn*. 'ayn' implies two of something, as in the famous World War Two battle at El-Alamayn (two flags). So *bahrayn* (Bahrain) means 'two seas' (Chapter 14).

To the east, I scanned across the tanker-filled strait to mainland Iran, searching for the summit of a conspicuous mountain seventy-five kilometres or forty nautical miles (NM) away, while endlessly to the south, the mountain peaks of the *ru'us al-jibal* faded in darkening purple ranks towards the Emirate of Fujairah. I returned to this coast some quarter of a century later when Omani hydrographic specialists, now armed with the latest satellite-based systems, were conducting the definitive survey of the area, and again five years after the millennium when maritime developments created the need for more aids to navigation (Chapter 24). On each occasion I had been struck by the history of this maritime gateway, one of the world's greatest waterways, the Strait of Hormuz, through which about a fifth of the world's oil and gas requirements is transported and which Alexander the Great's Cretan admiral Nearchus had sailed through as he passed into the Gulf via Cape Mazoon.

The control of this strait and that of its western cousin at the southern entrance to the Red Sea, the *bab al-mandeb* (*bab* means 'gateway') has never ceased in importance, but control must generally be exercised at sea by mariners with the means to do so. Those ashore can be frustratingly constrained as General Uqbah bin Nafi found in the seventh century CE. In 682, Bin Nafi led what Glubb termed a 1,500-mile *bedu* super-raid along the North African coast. He rode triumphantly into the Atlantic surf and brandishing his sword cried out, *'allahu akbar*! If my course were not stopped by this sea, I would ride on to the unknown kingdoms of the West.'

The sea passage from the head of the Gulf, through the strait, into the Gulf of Oman and beyond has been sailed by mariners for millennia, not all of them strictly historic. The opening to *'The First Voyage of Sindbad the Seaman'* in Sir Richard Burton's nineteenth-century unexpurgated translation of *alf laylah wa laylah* –*The Thousand Nights and One Night'* is, 'So, taking heart, I bought me goods, merchandise and all needed for a voyage, and impatient to be at sea, I embarked, with a company of merchants, on board a ship bound for Bassorah.' Sindbad (meaning 'a traveller to Sindh' – a province of what is now Pakistan) allegedly made seven voyages in all. On one, in Burton's translation, he encountered 'a fish like a cow which bringeth forth its young and suckleth them like human beings, and of its skin bucklers are made'. Sea-grass (*hashish*) eating dugongs (*'arus al-bahr* – 'brides of the sea') are found in large numbers both in the Gulf and the *ghubbat hashish* (Bay of Grass) near the island of Masirah.

On his second voyage he landed on 'a certain island [where] dwelleth a huge bird, called the "roc" which feedeth its young on elephants'. It is most likely that Arab mariners returning from East Africa had seen the *Aepyornis*, or elephant bird, on Madagascar. This voyage started at Bassorah (Basra), where Sindbad found a 'fine tall ship, newly builded, with gear unused and fitted ready for sea. I bought her and hired a master and crew, over whom I set certain of my slaves as inspectors. After reciting the *fatihah* [the first chapter of the Quran], we set sail over Allah's pool in all joy and cheer, promising ourselves a prosperous voyage and much profit'. Allah's pool (the Gulf) was the first of the Arab 'Seven Seas', which they then called *bahr faris* (Persian Sea). Unlike Sindbad, few if any Arabs refer to it by its formal geographical title 'the Persian Gulf' today.

A similar voyage was made in the mid-eighth century CE from the Gulf of Oman to an island which the Arabs called *sarandib* (Sri Lanka). This is the derivation of our word 'serendipity' – an unplanned fortunate discovery. They were delighted to find that it 'containeth many kinds of rubies and other minerals, and spice trees of all sorts', before they sailed onwards through the Malacca Strait to *khanfu* (Canton). This journey was re-created by 'The Sohar Ship', built at Sur by Oman's Ministry of National Heritage and Culture in the late 1970s and sailed from Muscat to Canton in 1980 by a team led by Tim Severin. The vessel subsequently formed the centrepiece of a roundabout outside the Al-Bustan Palace Hotel in Musqat – *bustan* meaning a grove or garden.

The seas surrounding the 'Island of Arabia', as the Portuguese adventurer Alfonso de Albuquerque called it (Chapter 10), contain fishery, mineral and petrochemical resources, which have been increasingly used to meet the needs of mankind. From the seventeenth century onwards, coastal states recognised that resources within their waters should be theirs alone to exploit. They claimed a belt of water three NM wide, which they would defend if necessary, that being the maximum effective range of the cannon mounted in their coastal defences. All the seas beyond that three-mile limit were called 'international waters – free to all nations and belonging to none'. After World War Two, coastal states claimed increasingly wider offshore zones from 12 to 200 NM in which hydrocarbon resources particularly could be exploited for the national interest. This brought them into contention with neighbouring states. As early as the mid-1950s, the United Nations recognised that international agreement should be reached to standardise these claims, but it took almost thirty years to achieve that aim when The United Nations Convention on the Law of the Sea was finalised in 1982. It is known as UNCLOS 82 and became international law twelve years later. This set common limits for coastal states of 12 NM for their territorial seas and 200 NM for an Exclusive Economic Zone (EEZ) in which offshore resources could be legally exploited. Waters beyond the 200 NM limit were called the 'High Seas', themselves subject to a new UN treaty which started its journey to ratification in 2023.

UNCLOS also set out rules for adjacent coastal states to delimitate their common maritime borders out to 12 NM, based on the principle of equidistance from points on their low water lines, and for opposite states to establish the boundaries of their EEZ where the distance between them was less than 400 NM. I was involved in two of these maritime boundary negotiations in the last decade of the twentieth century. One was the demarcation between the EEZs of Oman and Pakistan. In the ocean depths between these proud maritime nations, home to sperm whales, green turtles and yellowfin tuna, lies a subterranean mountain range, the Owen Fracture Zone, which divides the Arabian Sea from the Indian Ocean. An optimistic Omani scheme to lay an oil pipeline to India across this active fault line between two continental plates to India proved, unsurprisingly, to be both too expensive and impracticable. The other negotiation was with Oman's westerly neighbour, Yemen.

Yemen became a united country in 1970 after almost thirty years of civil unrest between Saudi-allied North Yemen and Communist South Yemen. The historical border between the two states had always been a distinctive giant grey square boulder with a central crack in it called, predicably 'Split Rock'. It rests on a ledge at the foot of a mountain escarpment near the border village of Sarfayt some 60 NM west of Salalah. The land border agreement between Yemen and Oman had been fixed. The penultimate act before the EEZ limit was agreed was to delimitate the maritime border out to 12 NM, and this required an expert from Oman (in this case me) and his Yemeni counterpart, or at least that was the theory.

I waited with my driver at the newly-opened border post between the two countries three hours ahead of the local low water of a spring tide, when the rocks at the foot of the cliff on which our observations depended would be uncovered. I bore my letter of authorisation, a hand-held GPS receiver, two large-scale maps, sheaves of high-quality aerial photographs and a camera. Split Rock was just three kilometres to the south, accessed by a newly graded but very steep track whose sweeping curves cascaded seawards. We needed to be there one hour before low water. We waited. And waited. With just an hour to spare, from the rapidly opening door of an ancient, rusty and dust-covered Toyota Landcruiser bearing broken Yemeni plates sprang a worried-looking youth clutching his letter and nothing else. He had only recently joined the Hadhramaut regional office of the land survey department of the appropriate ministry and had been told the day before to get to the border, where he would be briefed by an Omani officer. He was not expecting a six-foot-four Englishman wearing camouflage uniform bearing the three gold stripes of a *muqaddam bahry* (Commander) on his shoulder.

He need not have worried. We shared sufficient Arabic and English for him to understand the task in hand, he in his far-from-pristine *dishdasha* robe and me, by then in equally grubby trousers, sat on the edge of Split Rock, legs dangling above the waves a hundred metres below. With our aerial photographs in hand, we decided which rock was whose before ringing them on the images with magic markers. He was happy and so was I. Never has a border negotiation been so delightful or an initially nervous young surveyor been so relaxed. As we shared tiny cups of *kahwa* (coffee) back at the border post, he told me he came from Shibam, famed for its towering thirty-metre-high close-packed buildings, which Freya Stark noted rose out of the surrounding plain as if 'a cliff had wandered into the middle of a valley'. Before he clambered back into his Toyota with his annotated map and photographs safe in the leather wallet I had provided, he kissed me on both cheeks and told me he would never forget me. I am sure he has, but I will never forget him.

CHAPTER 3

ت   taa'
تاريخ   t'areekh

History

The Old Testament Book of Deuteronomy, Chapter 34 says that 'Moses went up from the plains of Moab unto the mountains of Nebo, to the top of Pisgah, that is over against Jericho.' When St Luke wrote that 'a certain man went down from Jerusalem to Jericho', he meant it literally. The road between the two drops 1,000 metres towards the Rift Valley floor at 403 metres below sea level, the lowest point on earth, where my father had built his bridge across the River Jordan. On a hot and dusty afternoon in June 2002, I stood on Mount Nebo and looked westward towards the head of the Dead Sea towards Jericho hidden in the haze over the River Jordan, then southwards towards the wilderness of Beersheba It was here that Ishmael, the supposed father of the Arabs, and his mother, Hagar, had, in a story common to Christians, Jews and Muslims alike, been saved from dying of thirst by the Angel Gabriel. My wife, Annie, and I had been driven to the summit by our taxi driver, Abu Tariq, a delightful, gentle and pragmatic Palestinian ex-businessman, who had lost everything after he was evicted from Kuwait City after the first Gulf War. Across the Jordan we could hear the sonic bangs from Israeli jets screaming above Jericho.

There was I, from Christian stock, reflecting on the plight of my Islamic host with the land of King David in the background. Three religions. One common deity. How had the sweep of history come to this? This chapter addresses briefly that story until the rise of Islam in the seventh century CE. The history of the successive Islamic Caliphates, Umayyads and Abbasids and their successors can be found elsewhere, but one renowned Pakistani academic observed that after the Abbasid dynasty splintered at the end of the ninth century, rival bedu tribes fell 'into a deep sleep from which they were to awake only in the late twentieth century'. Others, including myself, may disagree.

The Arabian peninsula was created between 800 and 200 million years ago, part of its mother, Gondwana. Tectonics moved the plate from tropical to southern polar regions and back again and progressively squeezed, submerged, silted and resurfaced it, such that it became a repository for the relics of countless shells, plants, and animals which were trapped beneath yet more protective oil- and gas-bearing sediments. Then thirty-five million years ago, the Arabian plate split from Africa creating a 2,000-metre-deep narrow trench – the Red Sea – between the two and crept north-eastwards to collide with Eurasia. Immense volcanic forces threw up huge drifts of volcanic basalt rocks, *harrat*, to litter the stone deserts of northern and eastern Arabia. The collision tipped the plate to raise a wind-sculpted mountain wall running the length of its ragged western edge – *as-sarawat*. Heat and wind erosion in these mountains provide the source for much of its sand in the central deserts. At its northern end stand the mountains of the Hejaz, brought so famously to the attention of the West by T. E. Lawrence. Its southern end flattens into the Tihama coastal plain, which runs south-eastwards, past modern-day Jeddah, off whose shores huge *hamur* (grouper) and myriad orange anthias fish compete for attention amid some of the best coral reefs in the world. From Mecca to Aden stretches the longest mountain range in Arabia, once thickly covered with juniper forest, home to hamadryades, baboons, and a few solitary *nimr* (leopards).

The collision also threw up Oman's eastern Al-Hajar mountain range (from *hajar* – 'stone'), as well as the Zagros mountains in Iran and the Makran range in Pakistan. To this day, the plate continues to move and tilt at about the annual rate that our fingernails grow as it undercuts the Eurasian Plate, leaving the deepest water in the Gulf on the Iranian side. Minor tremors are still felt in the Musandam Peninsula, which once caused the nineteenth-century glass lozenges in the lantern house of Didamar Lighthouse (Chapter 24) to crack and shatter.

At the height of the last great Ice Age, 20,000 years ago, a belt of temperate steppe ran along the south-eastern coast of the Mediterranean, across Mesopotamia and southwards into Arabia. With sea levels so depressed, what is now the Arabian Gulf was dry savanna, teeming with game. Examination of depth contours of modern charts show clearly where a large river valley ran down the Gulf, round the mountains which today contain the Strait of Hormuz and out into the precipitous depths of the Gulf of Oman.

Approximately 10,000 years later, temperature increases caused the Tigris and Euphrates to burst their banks and the sea level to rise rapidly over the low-lying Gulf regions, the likely derivation of Noah's flood. Archaeological excavations at Ur, that most ancient of cities 250 kilometres south-east of Babylon, revealed an eight-foot-thick layer of prehistoric alluvial clay. Evidence for a much wetter climate is revealed by the skeletons of hippopotamuses and water buffalo which lie beneath the Empty Quarter. After the heart of Arabia had dried out and the vast herds of gazelle and oryx had faded away, early plainsmen were forced to migrate towards the cloudy mountains or the distant alluvial plains of the major river valleys. The historian Paul Johnson in 'Civilizations of The Holy Land' tells us that they clashed with the indigenous Neolithic tribes who called them 'the horrors; the ghosts; the howling people; the long-necked men'.

It is hardly surprising that Old Testament and Quranic accounts of the flood are similar to those in the Mesopotamian epic of Gilgamesh: thousands of drowning disbelievers, an ark, a dove, a raven. Whatever their source, it was Noah's eldest son, Shem, from whom Abraham and all the semitic races are said to descend. The first of these included the Aramaeans, who settled in the area from Syria to Mesopotamia known as 'Aram of two rivers'. The second, the Canaanites, descendants of Noah's grandson, Canaan, included the Phoenicians – Homer's 'dark red

31

men' – who migrated through the Fertile Crescent to the Levant. For a long time they were the unsurpassed Mediterranean seafaring nation. They established their double-entrance stronghold ports of Sidon and Tyre and such was the strength of the fortifications at the latter that it took Alexander the Great seven months to breach its walls. It is said that he only stopped crucifying its inhabitants when he ran out of wood! According to Genesis, Canaanites comprised the whole pre-Israelite population, who were eventually overwhelmed by Hebrew invasions led by Joshua. The third group migrated to what is now Ethiopia, and the fourth were the so-called extinct tribes of Arabia. These included *al-'ad, ath-thamud, al-waber,* and *as-suhar.* Many districts of Oman still carry their names.

Early Arabian colonists included the Minaeans, who had settled in the Jawf area of north-eastern Yemen three to four thousand years ago. According to Wilfred Thesiger they became frankincense traders who worshiped a Moon God. Across the Empty Quarter, 18,000 kilometres to the north-east, dwelt a complexity of tribes living in the shadow of the *jebal bani jabir* (mountain of the sons of the *jabir* tribe), which towers above the Omani coastal plain. On its high plateau lies not only the second largest subterranean chamber in the world, the *majlis al-jinn* – the meeting place of spirits, explored first in 1983 by the intrepid American W. Donald Davison Jr – but rows of perfectly preserved 4,000-year-old conical towers, sentinels which mark the final resting places of ancient kings who were carried up on litters from the *ash-sharqiyah* plain almost 2,000 metres below. These and the beehive-shaped necropolii at *bat,* some 250 kilometres north-west, are similar to the tombs near the Buraimi oasis at *al-ayn* (old word for 'well') and the Bronze Age settlement of *umm an-nar* ('mother of the fire') in the UAE. The earliest known Bronze Age dwelling in Arabia (5020 BCE) is in Qatar, and its close neighbour, Bahrain, contains over 150,00urial mounds dating from 4800 BCE to 3800 BCE.

According to the Old Testament, Arab Semites were descendants of the Biblical Joktan (*qahtan* in Arabic), whose thirteen sons were named as the founding tribes of Arabia. The ancient name for the Musandam region, Mazoon, comes from his descendent, Mazen bin Azd. The sixth son, Uzal, founded the city now called Sana'a. Another son, Yarab, eventually colonised the whole of Southern Arabia from Yemen to the Al-Hajar mountains of Oman. They became known as *yamani* – those who dwelt on the right (Chapter 1). One of their rulers, Himyar (The Red One from *hamra* – 'red'), founded two dynasties, the first of which was subjugated by the Persian King Cyrus (see below), but the other, with some significant interruptions, came to rule southern Arabia until the time of the Prophet Muhammed's birth.

Another of Qahtan's descendants, Il'ad Yalut, had his capital at Shabwa in the Hadhramaut. The first century CE book *'Periplus of the Erythraean Sea* (principally a navigation pilot book – 'periplus' in Greek literally means 'a sailing-around') is an account of the harbour at 'Cana' (*qana*) – modern-day *bi'r ali* in the Hadhramaut, where 'all the frankincense produced in this country is brought by camels to that place to be stored, and to Cana on rafts held up by inflated skins. Il'ad also founded the port of Sumhuram (Samhar) at *khawr ruri* near modern-day Salalah. The Greeks called the port 'Moscha'. I visited it in the early 1990s before it was turned into a very impressive tourist site. The half-excavated site of crumbling yellow sandstone stands on a low hill overlooking a lagoon backed by the escarpment of the *qara* mountains. The 2,000-year-old inscriptions recording its foundation are sensibly preserved behind glass, but it took no great leap of imagination to feel the pulse of a once thriving community still thrumming through its ruins.

Qahtan's son, Sheba, founded the Sabean Kingdom with his capital at Marib. It was from here that their fabled queen journeyed along the ancient caravan routes to Solomon's Jerusalem 'with a very great train, with camels that bear spices, and very much gold and precious stones', Glubb, in his masterly *The Great Arab Conquests*, says that this journey had less to do with romantic liaisons than the payment of tribute to ensure the security of the Sabaean caravans upon which Marib's economy depended. Some two hundred years later, Nebuchadnezzar (605 BCE to 562 BCE) had built the Hanging Gardens of Babylon for his Median wife, Amytis, who was homesick for the Median mountains of her youth. He gave way to Cyrus, whose unified Achaemenid empire extended from the River Oxus in the East and along the southern shores of the Caspian and Black Seas to Cyrene in North Africa. It included Yemen and the coastal zone of what is now Oman.

After the Macedonian Empire collapsed following Alexander's early death in 323 BCE, the old Persian empire re-emerged as the Seleucid then Parthian kingdoms. The long-term ebb and flow of successive imperial states, including Roman expansion from 200 BCE, and the trade routes which fed them, eroded older geographical boundaries and deposited a cultural silt throughout the Middle East in which Grecian influences, including their philosophy and language, took root, enriched by Persian, Arabic, and Oriental deposits. This complex regional admixture would later assist both the spread of monotheistic religions and the extraordinary rapidity of the Arab conquests (Chapter 6).

Major maritime and territorial trading routes brought renewed wealth to towns including Muza (Mokha – later famous for its coffee), Aden (which the Romans called *Eudaemon Arabia*), Palmyra (Tadmur), and the Nabatean Capital at Petra (Chapter 23). Palmyra became legendary under its intelligent and ambitious third century CE female ruler, Zaynab, called Zenobia by the Romans and Cenobie in Chaucer's *The Monk's Tale*. Her husband commanded Rome's eastern army, but after his death (rumoured to be mariticide) she declared independence from Rome. Emperor Aurelian sent her into exile in 272 CE.

Another earlier exile from Marib was Malik al-Azd, from the same tribal stem as the previously mentioned Mazen. His full name, reminiscent of Biblical Hebrew genealogies, was Malik bin Fahm bin Ghanim bin Dows bin Adnan bin Abdulla al-Azd. It is said that his reason for quitting Marib was a squabble over a troublesome dog but probably had more to do with a serious tribal feud. In any event he led his and other tribes on a remarkable journey through the Hadhramaut to Wadi Qalhat near Sur in Oman. He fought and defeated the Parthians, including their elephants, in two decisive battles and became the effective ruler of greater Oman, named A'man after the wadi which his tribe had originally come from. The capital of Jordan has the same name and Arabic spelling, both starting with that awkward ع sound from the letter *ayn*.

The Syrian-born Roman historian, Ammianus Marcellinus, said that Arabs south of 'Provincia Arabia' were a race 'whom we never found desirable either as friends or enemies'. But they were determined to safeguard the western caravan route through Yemen, and it was the same Emperor Augustus, who decreed that 'all the world should be taxed', dispatched an expeditionary force under Aelius Gallus, Prefect of Egypt, southwards to secure Eudaemon Arabia and with it the strategic narrows of Bab el-Mandab, which controlled the southern entrance to the Red Sea. The force ran out of drinking water before it reached the great Sabaean dam at Marib and so failed to achieve its aim. This ended further Roman attempts to annex Arabia, although the maritime Red Sea route continued to operate under Roman franchise.

The Roman Byzantium Empire and its great rival, Persia, had enjoyed the so-called 'Endless Peace' instigated in 384 CE and which lasted intermittently until Chosroes Parwiz invaded Byzantium territory in 602 CE, thirty-two years after Muhammad's birth. The astonishing success of the Arabian Conquests left both Jerusalem and Damascus firmly under Caliphate control. Jews returned to the former to revitalise their culture, albeit in a city in which Islam had stamped its unique identity. Tolerance was the order of the day. The three great monotheistic religions lived and worshipped side by side in a holy city (*al-quds*) which was controlled, but not dominated, by Islam. Sadly this short-lived equilibrium was shattered subsequently by Fatamid destruction, Seljuk expansionism and the First Crusade. Accounts of this ninety-year hiatus can be found elsewhere, but Arabs have a very long memory and the slaughter which followed the last event has never been forgotten.

Under the genius of Muhammad's leadership, Arabia had acquired that most un-Arab-like characteristic – a sense of identity beyond the tribe. Given such an identity and common purpose, the Arabs had founded an Empire which, within fifty years, had had no historic equal. Within two hundred years it had been established in Africa, Asia and Europe, where it had given hundreds of nationalities a common language and a spiritual code which lasts to this day. The Arab legacy in Spain is remarkable. It can be found in Spanish language and nomenclature, and in such wonders as the citadel of the thirteenth-century and fourteenth-century Nasrid dynasty – the Alhambra – the red [house] in Granada.

The heady mixture of Arabic and Eastern influences achieved its apogee during the caliphate of Harun al-Rashid bin Muhammad al-Mahdi (766 CE to 809 CE), famed forever through *The Thousand Nights and One Night* (*The Arabian Nights*) mentioned in Chapter 2. Harun was a contemporary of Charlemagne, to whom he sent an embassy in 798 CE together with the gift of a white elephant. Such a gift may not have been particularly welcome, as useless, notoriously difficult and expensive-to-maintain white elephants were given by the kings of Siam to courtiers whom they wished to ruin! Two centuries later, Arabia's greatest minds rescued the knowledge of ancient civilisations and then exported it to Europe, an act which would enable the West to have its Renaissance. Other chapters will examine just what an impact this had on our own Western history.

CHAPTER 4

ث   thaa'
ثور   thoor

Bull

The squat fort at Barka, seventy kilometres west of Muscat, was constructed in the late seventeenth century and originally plastered with a protective coating of *sarooj*, a combination of crushed stone and sand mixed into a lime-and-gypsum base. In 1992 it stood surrounded by plain rectangular one-storey houses, the air above them criss-crossed with ugly black power cables. One of my Arabic colleagues, Ali bin Rashid, a native of Barka, told me that the town's name is derived from *barakah* meaning 'blessing' or 'good fortune'. Others in our company, always keen to differ in the Arab way, said that it came from *baraka*, a place where camels are made to kneel down. I stood on a roof with them on a Friday afternoon watching a storm thunder over the *juzur ad-daymaniyat* (Daymaniyat Islands), one of my favourite sailing destinations, fifteen kilometres (8 NM) offshore. Delighting in the pun, Ali told me that Barka's name might have been derived from *barq*, 'lightning', which we could see dancing over the intervening waves.

The rain clouds passed and my hosts, dressed in their immaculate white gowns called dishdashas (the Arabic plural is strictly *dashadeesh*), took me by the hand to a waiting car to drive the short distance to the sweat-and-urine-soaked dirt-floored bull-fighting ring surrounded by a circular low concrete wall on the outskirts of town. It was not the vile spectacle so loved by Hemingway but a form of bovine sumo wrestling, where the only thing which gets hurt is the owner's pride! Clearly betting is forbidden, but money did seem to change hands, as winning bulls, so Ali told me with a smile, are 'sold' to a new owner.

The zebu humped bulls which performed for us so engagingly came in three classes, the smallest the height of a child's shoulder and the largest, weighing in at several hundred kilograms, the height of a man. They are led towards each other, nonchalantly chewing cud, until their eyes lock. Sometimes the sight is enough, and one potential opponent scampers off, its rope halter and disappointed owner leaving dusty trails in its wake. More commonly, they turn towards each other with massive heads lowered, lock horns and start pushing ferociously until one huge beast runs away having had quite enough of that, thank you! The exclusively male crowd, sitting in groups on the ground or lining the walls, whoop and applaud before the next pair of bovine contestants are led by their 'seconds' to the fight. I was the only 'white-eye' (a common Arabic name for Europeans) here that afternoon but returned to Ali's house (*bayt*) with his compatriots and a slightly sore wrist, having shaken the hands of every owner and spectator in the ground.

This horn-locked pushing contest can also be seen during the winter months in Fujairah, 220 kilometres up the coast in that segment of the United Arab Emirates which separates the bulk of Oman from its Musandam province. The fascination with *thoor* (bull) fights is said, somewhat apocryphally, to be a relic of early Minoan feats of agility such as leaping over a bull's horns. Apocryphal or not, I saw images of bulls and other animals ten years later in the wonderful Umayyad hunting lodge at Qusayr 'Amra, fifty miles east of Amman. Security concerns among tourists made it practically devoid of visitors. This was to my advantage, as it was easier to conjure up an image of seated musicians accompanying the *qasida*, the evening's epic poetry recital, given within its cushioned interior. Mosaics of astonishing complexity covered the floor, representing not only bulls but dancing women, birds of prey, and game of every description, most of it now long gone from the surrounding countryside.

The Arab love of hunting led to much of its prey being hunted to extinction. The last Asiatic lion was shot at the end of the nineteenth century. The Arabian cheetah disappeared within the last fifty years, though as I have reported earlier, a few leopards still cling to life in the Arabian mountains. The *dhabi*, or Arabian gazelle, were numbered in tens of thousands less than eighty years ago. During their annual migration they were hunted on foot or chased into the mouths of Y-shaped traps called desert kites. The arrival of aircraft, sports rifles and 4WD vehicles spelt their decimation. Now it is not unknown for well-to-do Arabs to fly off to Africa or the remote regions of the old Islamic Empire to hunt the preferred prey of falconers, the houbara (Macqueen's bustard), as well as gazelle and *arnab*, the desert hare.

There have been some imaginative breeding and conservation programmes, notably for the once ubiquitous white Arabian oryx (*maha*), which was hunted to extinction by the early 1970s. It is said fancifully that these magnificent antelope, with their pair of scimitar-shaped horns, are the derivation of the unicorn, for when viewed side on they appear to have but one. They were almost extinct until reintroduced to Saudi Arabia, Israel, the UAE, and Jordan a decade later from captive individuals in private collections and zoos. The first major reintroduction programme was started in Oman's central gravel plain, *jiddat al-harasis*, in 1982, the year I sailed south to the Falklands War. By the time I was posted to Oman nine years later, a viable herd had been released from their pens to make their way in the wild. The cohort comprised some 400 individuals when I visited them in 1996. This success story was distinguished by the Arabian Oryx Sanctuary being granted listed status on the UNESCO World Heritage List.

However the best-laid plans, to paraphrase Burns, often go awry. The sand-and-gravel plain which the oryx called home lies above the majority of Oman's oil and gas reserves. With an expanding population and no other natural resources, the government expanded its hunt for petrochemicals into the reserve area. UNESCO unsurprisingly withdrew Oman from its list in 2007 when I was back in Oman for the third time, working as a civilian for the Sultan's cousin as general manager of one of his companies. By that time the wild oryx population had dropped to less than one hundred, driven downwards not through lack of grazing but by that insatiable but so-short-sighted Arabic love of hunting. To protect and indeed increase what was left of the herd, two successful oryx breeding centres have been established, one on the gravel plain called the Al Wusta Wildlife Reserve and the other near the capital. But the chance of these animals being released into Oman's wilderness is not good.

Wild animals, like the *bedu*, are no respecters of borders. To the Western eye, a map drawn up with neat linear boundaries gives a sense of security and order. Many straight-line borders existed in the peninsula before the first major oil strike was made in Bahrain in 1932. These were a legacy of European divisions created for political ends in the early twentieth century, as anyone familiar with the 1913/1914 Blue, Violet, Red, and the 1916 Sykes-Picot lines will confirm. The concept of formal territorial division had little meaning to Arabs. As the fourteenth-century historian and philosopher Ibn Khaldun noted, 'they have no walls or gates', only boundaries established by the seasonal wanderings of tribes as they followed the rains. The European concept of defined borders was traditionally alien, and many Arabs felt that linear boundaries had been forced upon them by nations who did not understand their local culture.

While Britain and France were secretly agreeing the division of their spheres of influence in Syria and Palestine, Prime Minister Balfour's ill-considered announcement on 9 November 1917 of British support for the concept of a Jewish National Home in Palestine was greeted with stunned disbelief by his Arab allies. This led Glubb to comment that 'there is little in all this to make an honest British heart feel proud, the story being largely one of muddle, mismanagement, duplicity and on occasions downright deceit'. Pragmatism eventually had its way. Both territorial and maritime borders are now part of modern life in the peninsula, mostly because of the resources that they demarcate. Petrochemicals will continue to be extracted and the oryx will continue to be contained. Mankind will continue to exploit both. Perhaps a greater focus on global reduction of the carbon footprint and preservation of the High Seas mentioned in the previous chapter will make my grandchildren's world a better place for them and their children.

There is of course hope and often joy. I encountered many species of mammal during my Arabian adventures. I surprised a pair of black Brandt's hedgehogs when following a rock-strewn trail in the Dhofar mountains at dusk. They are given to springing up under the bellies of their rare potential predators, so the local *al-hakli* (Qara) tribesmen, with whom I was camping, call them *qunfudh*, 'the jumping ones'. One of my hosts had the scars on his upper leg (don't ask) to testify to the effectiveness of their protective spines. On the same trip, and elsewhere, I heard the howls of the Arabian wolf (*dhib*), which range over the *jebel* in nightly patrols of up to fifty kilometres. The red fox (*al-tha'alab al-ahmar*) is common near Ra's al Hadd and it being unaware of the local Islamic dietary guidance, unwary Western campers better hide their food supplies, particularly bacon and sausages, or there will be no breakfast in the morning.

On the edge of the *al-huqf* escarpment on the eastern side of the vast acacia- and gazelle-studded *al-jiddat al-harasis* stand *ghaf* (prosopis) trees, half-buried by the serried ranks of sand dunes, which run to the sea. Strewn across the desert near the escarpment lie drifts of petrified bivalves, an ancient reef frozen in time. This is home to the rare Nubian Ibex (*al-wa'al*), which sadly has always eluded me. Luckily at the very foot of the cliff I came across a natural upwelling of water, no bigger than a cereal bowl, around which were the unmistakable prints of a medium-sized cat – the powerful, solitary, black-tufted-eared caracal (*al-washaq*). I never saw one either, but I bet it saw me!

One of the most enchanting animals in this region is the nocturnal Reuppell's sand fox with its soft, dense fur, white-tipped tail, and huge ears. We encountered them on the Barr al-Hickman plain opposite Masirah and again at sunrise driving slowly while following a family of oryx crossing the *jiddat al-harasis*. They were as surprised, but less delighted, as we were, with the two kitten-sized cubs, ears as large as their bodies, staring at us until their mother said, as did the defeated bull in Barka, 'Come now, that is quite enough of that!'

CHAPTER 5

ج   jeem
جمل   jamal

Camel

There is an apocryphal tale in which a French army officer, during the Napoleonic invasion of Egypt in the early nineteenth19th century, asked a man leading a camel what it was called. They thought he replied 'kamal' and so the name entered European vocabulary. This is of course nonsense. The Romans named them *camelus* and the Greeks *kamelos*, both from the Phoenician *gamal*. The primary Arabic word for camel is *jamal*. There are others, *ba'aeer* and the plural *a'abeel*, for example. What the long-suffering Egyptian meant was that the *name* of his camel was 'kamal' meaning 'perfection'.

There is no such thing in Arabia as a wild camel. All are owned by someone and most are named, like the Omani thoroughbred *Umbrausha*, which Thesiger rode in preparation for his first crossing of The Sands. Owners can distinguish the shape of an individual's hoofprint from amongst hundreds of others. Indeed there are dozens of words for the shape of a camel's hoof and a great raft of specific words for the various conditions and characteristics of these animals. For example a female camel is *in-na'aqa*. The pre-Abrahamic Arabian prophet Salih, whose tomb is said to lie near the village of Hasik in southern Oman (chapter 22) was said to miraculously make a pregnant female emerge from the mountainside when threatened by the idolatrous Thamud tribe. Other examples of camel descriptors are *al-jafool* (a camel prone to fright) and *al-ha'arib*, a female camel which walks ahead of a herd by such a distance that it appears to be running off!

Early ancestors of the Arabian single-humped camel (camelus dromedarius) – not to be confused with its Asiatic cousin, the twin-humped Bactrian camel – crossed the Beringia land bridge which connected the North American and Siberian plates about seven million years ago. Camel bones have been found in archaeological excavations dating from about 2400 BCE and had been in Arabia for some 3,500 years before that. Dromedaries were used as pack animals in the early Iron Age (1200 BCE to 100 BCE). The bones of domestical camels have been discovered dating from around 930 BCE. This ties in with Bernard Lewis's statement in his book 'The Middle East' that they were domesticated in the second millennium BCE and could carry 'up to 120 pounds, cover 200 miles in a day and travel for seventeen days without water'.

Camels, with their soft splayed hooves, were the only effective means of travel through the ancient desert. Horses were not introduced until much later. Camels have efficient mechanisms for withstanding extremes of temperature, retaining water and countering dehydration. A 600-kilogram adult can hoover up 200 litres of water in three minutes. Their leathery mouths protect them from the thorns of the acacia tree to which they are very partial. They can seal their nostrils and have a third eyelid to dislodge sand which gets stuck in their eyes. They can sprint at up to sixty-five kilometres per hour (km/h), sustain 40 km/h on good ground, and, so Thesiger reported, were a comfortable ride at a more normal 10 km/h. The problem came when they walked, which he noted 'threw a continuous and severe strain on the rider's back'. This was not a problem for the tiny six-year-old Pakistani children whom I saw being literally 'velcroed' onto their saddles before the camel races held in the last year of the millennium when I was based in the British Consulate in Dubai. That exploitative practice has now stopped, but I have lasting memories of these tots on their towering mounts galloping flat out with the owners racing their top-of-the-range Toyota Landcruisers one-handed whilst screaming at these children from the other side of the safety barrier.

Only Arab tribes bred camels, the stronger of which tribes maintained a monopoly over their use, providing guards and hiring camels to the caravan captains. They were excellent fighting platforms, but it was hard to stay mounted on a single-humped dromedary at speed, so miliary saddles were developed in the seventh century BCE. Horses are reputedly scared of the strong scent generated by a full-grown camel and so camel corps, or *dromedarii* as the Romans called them, were sometimes deployed in warfare against horse-mounted cavalry. Both horses and camels saw action in the battles described in the next chapter.

Thoroughbred camels, like horses, have always been admired for their grace and beauty and camel beauty contests are big business in Saudi Arabia, Qatar and the UAE, where perfectly formed humps and lips can win owners of these contestants not inconsiderable sums. The total prize money at one of these festivals in 2022 was over £10 million, with the most beautiful winner (or rather its owner) being awarded £200,000. Indeed such is the value of these prizes that unscrupulous owners have been known to use Botox to enhance appearances. The hides of these animals are valued too. Camel hair comprises an outer guard layer and a softer undercoat. The former provided material for *bedu* tents while the latter clads Europeans in expensive coats.

And if coats and beauty contests were not enough, they are good to eat too! Consumption of camel meat is considered *halal* ('allowed'). That from a young dromedary is prized particularly highly in Arabia where, being quite tough, it is boiled slowly then served heaped on a huge bed of rice, flavoured with tomato and sprinkled with fried onions, garlic, nuts, and dried fruit. Occasionally, along with lamb and goat, camel meat is smothered in a spicy mixture of cardamon, cloves, and cumin before being wrapped in palm or banana leaves, inserted in a cloth bag and then baked in an earth oven. This is the renowned *shuwa* feast, more common in Oman then elsewhere in the Gulf, and is gastronomic perfection personified. Frothy, rich camel milk is good too and has sustained the *bedu* for centuries. It has been said that a single tribesman can survive on camel milk alone for a lunar month.

The other animal feted in Arabia is the horse. Because of their rarity and fame in Arab poetry and legend, they acquired considerable status, such that, together with falcons and slaves, they could form part of the tax paid to Islamic rulers. Horseracing is now the sport of *shaykh* as well as kings, and some of the finest horses come from the Al-Maktoum Godolphin stable. It was named after that famous 'Arab' stallion, though in fact the horse in question had been imported from France, where it had been gifted by the Bey of Tunis. A tradition has persisted that a pure (*asil*) Arabian blood line has been maintained to the present day from horses bred by *bedu* in the highlands of the Nejd and by *bani battash* tribesmen living on the watered gravel plains north of Oman's Wahibah Sands.

I witnessed *ja'alan* horse races held near Ibra, where two superb horsemen would gallop together at full tilt, each gripping the outstretched arm of the other. Great horsemen they certainly are, but the idea of an unadulterated bloodline is just a myth. The horse is a creature of the steppes and was not common in Arabia until the seventh century CE, although ancient horses, such as Hipparion, had roamed the river valleys of the peninsula until they dried up. Their hooves are unsuited to soft desert sand and, unlike the camel, they need regular supplies of fodder and good-quality water. They were rarely harnessed to a plough, wagon or water-wheel but were used for show and hunting. Following the conquests, the *bedu* increased their herds by exploiting the extensive new *d'ar* available to them.

Chapter 13 recounts how horses were bred and fattened in the Dhofar region of Oman before being shipped, with sufficient feed, up the coast to *wadi qalhat* just to the north-west of Sur. Here they were kept safe in the steep-sided narrow-mouthed *wadi* in their thousands before being shipped on the north-east monsoon to India. The seventeenth-century Portuguese occupiers of Eastern Arabia, focused on the rigorous enforcement of their commercial advantage, issued a ban on horse breeding and trading, but this tradition outlived them. Three centuries later I was invited to become the English commentator for the winter show-jumping season held at As-Sib west of Musqat, where riders from the *ja'alan* and *sharqiyah* regions swept round and sometimes even over the multi-coloured jumps in the exquisitely manicured grounds of Sayyid Shabib's showground, while the band of the Royal Guard played Western music and guests were served tea in china cups and cucumber sandwiches. I could not make this up!

Every Wednesday afternoon (Wednesday – *al-arba'a* – is counted as the fourth day of the week) I mounted the commentators' stand with my Omani female counterpart, and after the standard formal introduction, I broadcast a welcome – *ahlan wa sahlan* – to the assembled company. His Highness, who had a wicked sense of humour and a beautiful Austrian wife, encouraged me to provide understated but cutting commentary on riders who scattered the poles with their shoulders as they flew headlong off their mutinous mounts. Knowing that my undeserved criticism was only for HH's enjoyment, the riders, many of them from the Royal Guard, forgave me my rudeness, particularly as few, if any, understood what I was saying. At the end of each season, Sayyid Shabib hosted a lunchtime party in his grounds to which riders, trainers, and commentators were invited. Having distributed gifts to all – a watch one year, newly-minted money another – we gathered in groups for the *fudhl*.

The wonderful word *tafadhal* with that difficult 'dtha' back-of-the-throat sound at its centre, means so much more than just 'Be so kind' or simply 'You are welcome'. It also means 'Come in, please!', 'After you, please!', 'Please, if you please!', 'Take this [gift], please!', the exclamation mark indicating the warmth and heartfelt nature of the invitation. And from this comes the name for a group meal, *fudhl* with the food in the centre and the (male) participants seated cross-legged on the ground around it. One eats with one's right (never left) hand by scooping up a handful of meat and rice then squeezing it into a deliciously greasy ball before stuffing it into one's mouth. Conversation is understandably suspended during this process. As soon as the meal is finished, coffee and dates taken, and fingers rinsed by a waiting servant, one is off. Hands are shaken all round before departure without another word being spoken apart from *ma'a salaama ya estef'n wa allah ma'ak* – 'Goodbye, O Stef'n and may God go with you'. The Almighty may well have done, because one year on the way home from such an event, a camel, perhaps one prone to flight, lolloped, tongue flapping, in front of my car. Brakes squealed and I just missed it. The vociferous owner, broken halter in hand, pursued his charge as it sent shopping trollies spinning into the parked vehicles in the supermarket car park across the road causing not insignificant damage. Imagine the wording on the insurance claims.

CHAPTER 6

ح   haa'
حرب   harb

War

During the Cold War against the Soviet Union, I served in two Royal Naval 'Ocean Class' hydrographic ships ploughing endless furrows in the deep North Atlantic, having previously gained some basic escape and evasion skills and a few 'get out of Russia free' phrases. But my first experience of hot war was as the second-in-command of HMS Hydra during the Falkands conflict. Other operations in Arabia such as HARLING and DESERT STORM followed, but the first conflict I witnessed first-hand was as a six-year-old living alongside the Palestinian refugee camp at Zerqa, just outside Amman in Jordan, when its occupants rose up in revolt in 1956. Defensive sand-bagged machine-gun posts were established on our garden wall facing the camp, and just before my mother and my siblings were evacuated to the UK via Rome, one of my father's best Arab Legion friends, another English half-colonel, was shot dead whilst trying to deal courteously with civil unrest.

War and its consequences have dominated Arabian history and continue to do so to this day. The power struggles between Pharaonic Egypt and Middle Eastern tribes, including the Hittites, who had sacked Babylon in 1595 BCE, are conjured up in Shelley's poem 'Ozymandias' (Pharaoh Ramesses II) with its famous phrase, "Look on my Works, ye Mighty, and despair!' Present conflicts in Palestine, Israel, Syria and Yemen have powerful third-party backers and tragically, it would seem, ongoing and heart-rending despair.

The word for war in Arabic is _harb_. It starts with a big aspirated 'H' sound, unlike the other aitch in Arabic, (ه) also pronounced haa but more softly. One eponymous Arab tribe, *al-ḥarb*, occupied a band of territory from the Red Sea coast near Jeddah north-eastwards towards what is now Kuwait. With delegated responsibility for urban security, they acted mercilessly on behalf of the merchant clan which controlled pre-Islamic Mecca and subsequently to drive weaker *bedu* tribes back into the desert. Later some *al-ḥarb* intermarried with those of African descent and thereby lost true *bedu* status. They became virtual outlaws and subsequently fought on the side of the Ottoman Turks in World War One, eventually to be put down by *al-'ikhwaan* (The Brotherhood). These puritanical 'roving, ravening' marauders were described as 'the white terror of Arabia' They became Abdul-Aziz Ibn Saud's stormtroopers, used to confuse, surprise, or terrify his opponents. In 1924, Ibn Saud, who Sir John Glubb said, 'would have ended up as prime minister in any country in the world' let loose *al-'ikhwaan* on Taif in the Hejaz, not far from Mecca. The *sherif* (guardian) of the Holy Places abdicated and Ibn Saud became their ruler, a role the House of Saud maintains to this day. The story behind why these places became known as 'Holy Places' started in the early seventh century CE as a conflict between the followers of a troublesome young prophet and the dominant *al-quraysh* clan in the historic market town of Mecca, confluence of caravan convoys for centuries.

One of the consequences of the birth of Islam was that previous tribal allegiances and rivalries were, at least in theory, to be replaced by a unifying Islamic family (*ummah*), initially a group of a few hundred with Muhammad as its 'sheikh' but one which would grow into what Karen Armstrong in her 'A History of God' called 'a super-tribe' a community or brotherhood which as of today forms one fifth of the world's population. One of Muhammad's revelations was that the *ummah* had a sacred duty to fight non-believers. These included, of course, *al-quraysh*, who during Muhammad's twelve-year ministry there had pelted him with stones and rubbish, placed thorns under his feet and finally planned his assassination.

Adherence to this unified family took, as the Christian Arabist, Alfred Guillaume, put it, 'precedence over all other ties and relationships, so that a believing father might have to slay an unbelieving son'. The sacred duty to achieve God's will was called *jihad*. The word *jihad* has no inherent relationship to war. It is a struggle to improve the world, a concept of inner peace which cannot be achieved if faith is threatened or the Islamic code of social justice is violated. The Quraysh had violated this code, so *jihad* was justified. In January 624 CE, Muhammed, now the leader of his base in Yathrib (later renamed in his honour *medinat an-nabi* – the city of the prophet – Medina), intended to remind them of this by attacking a southbound thousand-camel caravan train laden with goods for the great Meccan pilgrimage market, protected, so he thought, by only about thirty armed guards – no match in his estimation for his 319-strong force. His estimation proved to be wrong.

The caravan route through *biir al-badr* – the wells of Badr – ran just 130 kilometres to the west of Medina. The *mukowweem* – the caravan captain's early-warning network of outriders and informers – had got word of the raiding party and had sent riders ahead to ask for reinforcements from Mecca. This intelligence included the fact that two riders had recently watered their camels at the wells, and forensic examination of their droppings revealed date stones from a species peculiar to Medina. As for names of camel hoofprints, different date varieties had unique Arabic names. Thus forewarned, the camel train turned towards the coast and reached Mecca unmolested. But riding towards Badr was a Meccan force, so Glubb tells us, of 'seven hundred and fifty camel riders and a hundred horsemen clad in chain mail.

When the two forces met, they called a council of war, followed by an initial clash of champions redolent of Macaulay's Lays of Ancient Rome. The sun and sand were in the eyes of the Quraysh, which gave Mohammed's inspired warriors a significant advantage. In the ensuing melée, young men, certain of paradise, threw themselves into the ranks of the Qurayshi. The

Meccan army, lacking in miliary disciple and spiritual fervour were routed; forty-nine of them lay dead and a further fifty were ransomed. Muhammad's inferior force at the Battle of Badr had been outnumbered three-to-one but returned to Medina with the spoils of war, having gained a victory which, surah 8:9 of the Holy Quran declared, was aided by 'a thousand angels'.

To put the date of the next event into historical context, 625 CE was the year that Paulinus was consecrated bishop in Canterbury before heading northward to convert King Edwin of Northumbria. In Arabia that year, the Quraysh intended to wreak their revenge. A force of three thousand rode out of Mecca, bound for Medina. Imagine the sight. Seven hundred helmeted men in chainmail bearing their principal weapon of war, the heavy razor-edged sword, mounted on camels with huge war banners streaming overhead. Horsemen, hundreds of them armed with lances. Archers and mercenaries, including specialist javelin throwers. If that were not enough, following behind came the chieftains' wives, borne on beribboned camel litters, exhorting their warriors to fever pitch with ululations and ritual tossings of their long black hair.

Scouts brought news of the approaching army. Medina was not a fully fortified town, rather a cluster of walled enclosures, each capable of defending itself but not of participating in a co-ordinated action against such a large force. Muhammad could muster about seven hundred defenders, including fifty archers whom he planned to use to protect his left flank. Battle was joined next morning, starting with single combat engagements. With cries of *allahu a'kbar* – 'God is the Greatest' – drowning out the ululations of the Qurayshi women, the faithful fell on the Qurayshi frontline with such ferocity that they appeared to be winning the day, but as at the Battle of Senlac (Hastings) 441 years later, the tide was to turn. Muhammad's archers, thinking that their defensive role was over, commenced looting the Qurayshi fallen. Seizing the opportunity, two hundred Qurayshi horsemen swept round them and literally decimated Muhammad's force. Seventy were killed for the loss of only twenty Quraysh. The faithful fled to the protection of Mount Uhud, after whom the battle was subsequently named, and watched helplessly as their enemy plundered the field of battle. One of the dead was Muhammad's uncle, taken out by a mercenary javelin thrower, hired by the daughter-in-law of a man killed at Badr. Having found his body, she slit it open and ritually ate part of his raw liver!

A year later, the Quraysh determined to defeat their troublesome northern neighbours once and for all. They assembled a force of about ten thousand, comprising four thousand Quraysh supported by six thousand from allied tribes, and rode in a great dusty column towards Medina. But Muhammed and his followers had not been idle. A fortified earthwork had been constructed to protect the exposed northern side of the town, as had a defensive ditch. The ditch, after whom the subsequent battle was named, confused the invaders, who initially attempted no full-scale attack. Impatient for action, four intrepid Qurayshi horsemen cleared the ditch at full gallop, the leader throwing down the gauntlet of single combat, which (much to his surprise, rather like Horatio's opponent, Lausulus of Urgo) he lost – cut down by a single sword stroke. His companions skuttled back across the ditch to safety. The siege continued, but due to poor logistical planning, the Qurayshi camels started dying for lack of fodder. The final straw which broke all their backs was a storm, a great dust-gathering wind, a mighty *jinn*, which blew on the twelfth night and flattened the Qurayshi encampment. The demoralised force headed for home or melted back into the Nejd desert.

Muhammad's dominance was now complete. A ten-year truce was agreed with *al-quraysh* and his fame spread. Tradition has it that in 629 CE he sent letters and embassies to the rulers of the two great rival powers of Byzantium and Persia and to the kings of Yemen and Abyssinia, enjoining them all to embrace the new faith. The story of the rest of his life and of the subsequent Arabian Conquests has been told brilliantly elsewhere, but his legacy remains with us to this day, as do, sadly, continuing conflicts on the Arabian Peninsula, which seem set to end no time soon. The italicised quotation shown below from the Royal Commission looking into the root cause of the 1936 Palestinian rebellion was written eighty-seven years ago but remains as true today. The commission considered the cause to be 'the Arabs' wish for their independence [from Britain] *and the fear of the Jewish National Home*' (my italics).

A second quotation from seventy years ago is no less dated. In July 1951, King Abdullah of the Hashemite Kingdom of Jordan was assassinated by an Arab extremist as he entered the Great Mosque in Jerusalem. Following the abdication of his son Talal, Hussein bin Talal was crowned king in November 1953. It was on his knee that I sat three years later. Just after his coronation, Jordan's prime minister was asked if there would ever be a solution to the Israeli/Palestinian problem. 'Of course,' he replied, 'but it will take time' When asked how much time he said, 'Well, not time as you might chose to define it. I am thinking of four or five hundred years.'

CHAPTER 7

خ   khaa'
خيمة   khayma

Tent

In the summer of 1984, reports of shipping being damaged by mines came in from the Gulf of Suez. Some of these were clearly false, as the reported explosions created holes in ships' sides with the steel bent outwards rather than inwards, somewhat surprising for damage caused by munitions external to a vessel, but a hopeful, if bogus insurance claim nevertheless! Others though were genuine, and in response to a request from the Egyptian government, a task force of specialist Royal Navy minehunters set sail from their base on the River Clyde, Suez-bound. I was the staff navigator of the Rosyth-based small ships' 'Work Up' organisation tasked with evaluating and improving the military capabilities of these vessels. I could also speak some Arabic so was sent to Adabiyah at the southern end of the Suez Canal. My orders were to provide a shore-based precise navigation chain for the minehunting and clearance task code-named OPERATION HARLING. I knew I would need to coordinate some sites on both sides of the Red Sea using high-precision satellite receivers, so I contacted a local army base to source the necessary support equipment. A slightly rotund and nearing retirement major of the Royal Logistic Corps welcomed me without enthusiasm, but when I told him my requirements his eyes lit up. 'Tentage, eh?' he spouted. 'Well, my lad, you are in luck.' And so it provided to be, for tents he had in their thousands. To his intense disappointment, I left with only two.

The Author with Egyptian Soldiers during OPERATION HARLING

khayma is the Arabic word for tent. The derivation of the name of the United Arab Emirate Ra's al-Khaimah comes from Arab mariners who recognised their landfall because the shape of one of its distinctive mountains from seaward resembled the peak (head – *raas*) of a *bedu* tent, their shelter from the sun since they had first made the desert their home. Within a shaded shaykh's tent was an open-sided carpeted meeting place, or *majlis*. Doughty called it the 'coffee-parliament of an Arab Prince'. This is where guests were served coffee and dates – *tamr*. Fresh dates harvested half-ripe in the humid (*ratab*) summer months are called *rutab*. The lower end is dark brown and sweet, the end nearest the stalk, beige and crunchy. The combination of tastes and textures bears no comparison to the densely packed objects available in Western supermarkets at Christmas. I have often asked my Arab interlocutors whether their word for humidity comes from the time when dates start to ripen or whether the date gives its name to the weather phenomenon. I have yet to have the definitive answer and remain in sweet ignorance.

Dates imported in considerable quantity from Musqat and the Gulf have always sustained the inhabitants of the Dhofar coast. Captain Haines noted in his mid-nineteenth-century journal that if a naval blockade of this trade (estimated to amount to some 25,000 tons during the November to December north-east monsoon season) were instigated, it could create a famine along that coast. When he mentioned this to some of the more intelligent import merchants, they were astonished that anyone would consider such a thing, one disclaiming 'that is not the idea of a man but of the devil. Say no more about it, for dates are bread, and bread is the staff of life'. Haines noted that the larger of the trading vessels which had carried dates to Dhofar returned 'after the first blast of the south-west monsoon had been felt, loaded principally with coffee.

The English word 'coffee' comes originally from the Arabic word *qahwa*, derived from the verb *qawaa*, which means to strengthen or fortify. This became *kahwe* in Turkish, then *koffie* in Dutch. Legends tell of a ninth-century East African monk called Chadely or Scyadly hearing of the stimulating properties of the bean of *coffea arabica* from a local (some say Arab) goatherd called Kaldi. His fellow monks tried this new crushed berry drink and found that they could remain awake during night prayers with no loss of intellectual reason. By the end of the following century, *qahwa*, or the 'drink that fortifies' became known as the Muslim Wine, because strict adherents, forbidden from drinking alcohol, used coffee as a substitute. Rather than wine putting them to sleep, the faithful drank *qahwa* to sustain themselves while emulating the Prophet's practice of sleeping little in order to pray.

The Naval Prayer entreats that sailors 'may return in safety to enjoy the blessings of the land with the fruits of our labours'. Sindbad certainly did, applying himself 'to all manner of joys and solaces and delights, eating the daintiest viands and drinking the deliciousest wines'. Wine and its links to love feature prominently in Arabic poetry. It would be offered in Paradise, albeit in a non-intoxicating form. Earthly alcohol, from *al-kohl* (the powdered antimony used in the east to stain the eyelids) was considered to be an abomination devised by Satan, as was gambling. Wine was therefore denied to believers but not to *dhimmi* (non-Muslims living in an Islamic state), which is why it is served today in hotels and restaurants in many Gulf countries. Wine was originally obtained secretly from its expert vintners, the Christian monasteries of ancient Arabia, or fermented far from the public eye. Persian emigrants from Shiraz brought their knowledge of viniculture to the mountains of Oman, where trellised vines can be found to this day high on the terraced gardens (*bustaan*) of the Jebel Akhdar mountains. Excessive alcohol consumption was reported by Lorimer to be a factor during a British naval engagement with the Dutch off Jask in 1654. 'The Dutch were most of them drunk, and knew not what they did; the English I think were little better, if not worse'!

At some time after the eleventh century, a perhaps accidental discovery found that an improved beverage could be obtained by roasting coffee beans. Word of coffee's properties spread northwards along the *hajj* route to Damascus. The first coffee house, the Kiv Han, run, so Lewis tells, us by two Syrians, opened in Constantinople in the late fifteenth or early sixteenth century. One of them came from Aleppo and returned there three years later with a profit of five thousand gold pieces. The popularity of these centres of entertainment and discussion was such that coffee houses became known as the 'Schools of the Wise'. Sporadic attempts to ban its consumption generally failed. It is said that in 1511 the Mamluk governor of Mecca, Khair Beg, was executed for banning coffee in a futile attempt to prevent opposition to his corrupt rule. Such was its success that by the early seventeenth century, green coffee beans were being imported by Venice and in 1650, the first coffee house was opened in Oxford, England, by an enterprising Turkish Jew.

The cloud-covered terraces above the Tihama plain, which Thesiger reported to be home to people of 'uncommon beauty' were found to be perfect for cultivation of the coffee shrub. From the late fourteenth century onwards, Yemen became increasingly the principal coffee-growing region, with the port of Mocha (Mokha) as its export hub. The Arabs maintained their control over the commodity by only permitting beans which had been sterilised by boiling or drying to be exported. However, like silk before it, market forces found a way of breaking the monopoly. In the late seventeenth century, the Dutch smuggled a parent plant out of Mocha and cultivated coffee in Sri Lanka and Java. Yemen's control was superseded. Fewer and fewer European ships docked in Mocha to load its increasingly expensive beans. Arab coffee merchants had priced themselves out of the export market and had to contend with local trade, where demand remained constant.

Supplies of the revered bean were carried and crushed in tinkling brass mortars by the nomadic tribes of the great deserts or left as an offering for others at the remote shrines of female saints such as Waila Riqaiya on the fringes of *ar-rub al-khali*. Thesiger reported this practice before his second crossing. He commented that the *is-saar* tribe, with whom he was camping, had a reputation for godlessness because they 'neither fast nor pray'. They flavoured their coffee strongly with ginger, serving it in a large earthenware cup to a recipient who was expected to take just a sip before handing it back to the server, who topped it up and passed it to the next person. Cardamon-flavoured *qahwa*, often accompanied by dates, is now served in small handle-less cups to guests who are expected to sip it noisily, accept a second pouring when offered then shake the cup to indicate that they have had enough. If the cup is not shaken, it will be endlessly refilled much to the amusement of one's host!

Arab hospitality is legendary, a fact attested to by Haines during his superb hydrographic survey of the Arabian Sea coast. One of his Arabic-speaking officers, Mr Smith, conducted a fact-finding expedition to the mountains above the Salalah Plain. In order to fit in, he called himself Ahmed. Staying in the tents of the local Gharrah tribe, he became their great favourite. 'In every instance,' he noted, they 'gave him the warmest place by the fire' and 'offered him a wife and some sheep, if only he would stay and reside with them.'

They urged him not to drink water from streams. 'No, Ahmed,' they said, 'do not return and say we gave you water while our children drank nothing but milk.' According to Haines, the blue-robed women who came to barter their cattle, butter, and gums (frankincense) for dates at the market in Mirbat (the site of an SAS battle in 1972) credited their noticeably good looks to drinking nothing but milk since childhood.

The seasonally arid mountains of Dhofar are transformed into misty and waterfall-filled valleys during the *kharif*, or southwest monsoon. So too are Freya Stark's 'high-shouldered mountains' of Yemen. Within such mountains lie breathtakingly beautiful palm- and oleander-filled wadis. Haines already knew that the river-less land of the Arabian Peninsula had been hard for early geographers to accept. The earliest Ptolemaic maps show rivers flowing to the sea near Jeddah, Ra's al-Khaimah, Qalhat near Sur, and the Hallaniyah islands east of Salalah. The last of these, *Fluvius Prim*, was still depicted with some confidence on a Dutch map dated 1792 CE. It might have been named after the village of Berim on the Hadhramaut coast (no Arabic 'p') but the derivation is not certain. In time these 'rivers' were shown as less dramatic wadi outfalls which flowed strongly into the sea after heavy rainfall. When walking through these wadis one encounters the ingenious and often complex network of irrigation channels imported into Oman from the Persian Achaemenian dynasty. These were enhanced when the Sasanids controlled eastern Arabia from the third to sixth centuries CE.

The Persian *qanat* system was based on digging a well to the water-table level at the foot of a mountain, then marking a course from that spring to the area or village to be watered. Vertical shafts were dug at intervals along this course before the shafts were connected by tunnels. The plural Arabic word for the *qanat* system is *aflaaaj*, which in its singular form (*falaj*) means 'cleft' or 'split into parts'. These systems maximise the use of what little ground water can be captured for cultivation and transport it through narrow aqueducts which cling to mountain slopes or dive underground through a syphon to re-emerge on the other side of a *wadi*. The fields fed by *aflaaaj* are filled to this day with exotic fruits and *naranj*, the bitter orange.

Arabic influence on Spain can be seen in the Spanish for 'orange' which is *naranja*. Limes (*leem*) flourish in Oman, as do *leemoon* (lemons), aloes, and rice (*ruz*). The Arabic for the sweet orange is *burtaqaal,* named after the race, the Portuguese, which introduced them into Arabia in the sixteenth century. The coast from Khasab to Sur, including the great green arc of the Batinah plain, bristles with seventeenth-century protective forts and reinvigorated palm plantations shading fields of alfalfa (lucerne) from the Arabic *al-fisfisa* – fresh fodder. Other names for food, fruit, and vegetables derived from Arabic include artichoke and cumin, jasmine and marzipan, saffron, sherbet and syrup, tarragon and tamarind.

Some *wadi* are despoiled by heedless littering from locals and ex-patriates alike and by the presence of ubiquitous blue plastic shopping bags which float on the air stirred up by swirls of dust. The date groves in them are home, in some locations, to malarial mosquitoes, carriers of Deuteronomy 28's 'extreme burning'. These are said to be *jinn* (demons). The swirling dust storms of the Arabian desert are still called *jinn* by the *bedu*. But good *jinn* (fairies) were created, so it was said, from the smokeless fire which stood between men and angels. Despite irritating mosquitoes, many expatriates look forward to weekend camping in these *wadi*, pitching their tents carefully on ground which is unlikely to flood if a sudden rain squall hits the mountains above. They light fires and tell tales long into the night, sparks circling skywards, fanciful fairies, perhaps. One of my favourite weekend sites was litter-less *wadi siq* in Oman, where after the dawn prayer on a Friday morning, a diligent and time-burnished Sudanese school master poured me tiny cups of cardamon-flavoured *qawha* from a battered thermos. He watched, smiling, as we sat side by side on the trunk of a fallen date palm as I taught the laughing children under his perfect care to tie imperfect knots using the parted ends of one of the guy ropes of my tent which had been chewed in half during the night, doubtless by an overly-inquisitive goat. A tent set in a date grove in a *wadi* watered by an ingenious *falaj* system, sharing coffee with delightful company. The very essence of Arabia.

CHAPTER 8

د   daal
دشداشة   dishdasha

Robe

One of the memorable delights of visiting Arabia, or indeed Istanbul or Marrakesh, is to head into the mouth of a covered souk (*suq*) and explore its maze of narrow passageways lined with stalls and glass-fronted shops clustered in categories: multi-coloured aromatic spices, leather goods, gold and silver jewellery, clothing, and in some cases, antique small arms and swords. One is assailed both by unique smells and the yells of vendors always keen for one's custom and cash. Bargaining is very much the order of the day, as most commodities other than food carry a mark-up of at least forty percent, often much more to obvious tourists. The negotiation starts with a smile as one asks, 'How much, please?' – '*kam min fadhlik*' – the last word literally meaning 'with kindness'. A price is given. After an appropriate pause indicating mild shock, one raises one's eyes, opens one's arms, palms upwards, and states incredulously, '*ghali jidda*' ('Very expensive!').

The vendor will smile as the bargaining process commences. The cost will start to fall accompanied by theatrical pleas of hardship from the seller until a mutually satisfactory bid is agreed upon. This performance is followed of course by much shaking of hands, and 'Come again. Bring your friends. I will always give you the very best price!'

The first shops at the entrance of the wonderful souk in Muttrah, the port in Musqat – meaning 'the place of setting down (cargoes)' – are tourist traps piled high with Indian-made tat. But a little further in, visitors are drawn to the stalls selling small embroidered and perforated circular traditional caps, *kuma,* worn by Omani men. They, the caps not the men, come in dozens of colours and designs, some of them very intricate. It is said that the *kuma* originated in Zanzibar, which was once an Omani Sultanate. Sultans and other members of Oman's Royal Family wear an elaborate turban, the *qraiat*, which came from the Persian coast. All others wear the *kuma*, a basic version of which costs just a few rials. The more elaborate ones with lace-like perforations to let in cooling air demand much higher sums.

The tailored robes which both Omani customers and vendors wear are procured from specialist shops lined ceiling-high with heavy swatches of the finest quality silky Egyptian and Indian cotton. This material makes the standard dress for males in Arabia – the *dishdasha* – a loose-fitting long-sleeved cotton robe, mostly white or pastel shaded and generally immaculately ironed. I had shirts made from the same material, and being over six feet tall, made-to-measure white cotton work overalls too, a luxury perhaps not found in the UK. The *dishdasha* is worn over an *ezar*, a patterned waist-to-ankle cotton wrap. Open-toed sandals complete the outfit. Many middle-class men carry a thin bamboo camel stick, very much like a headmaster's cane. I have only ever seen this wielded once in that manner by an irate father who had had quite enough of his son's impudence. Both doubtless lived to regret that loss of composure, a rare outburst in a land where public self-control is very much the order of the day.

One of my acquaintances who epitomised perfect manners was the Director-General of Ports and Maritime Affairs in the Omani Ministry of Transport and Communications. After thirty-five years' service, I had retired from the Royal Navy at the then compulsory age limit of my 52nd birthday and had spent a couple of years learning how to be a civilian. Having acquired that skill, I returned to Oman at the invitation of a member of the Omani Royal Family to be the general manager of a new company which exclusively supplied aids to navigation services to the Sultanate under a concession agreement with the government. This is covered in Chapter 24, but a strong relationship with the ministry and its director general was essential. This gentleman was a short, somewhat rotund and extremely astute individual, who sat behind a desk somewhat larger than an airfield. I like him enormously. Over his immaculate *dishdasha*, trimmed at the neck with a strip of blue embroidery, he wore a rectangular tunic called a *thaub* and a small circular turban (*massar*) over his *kuma*, the latter retaining the former's shape. This smart combination had the somewhat uncomfortable habit of hindering air circulation around his intelligent head. Although the airconditioned office was icy, his forehead was often beaded with droplets of perspiration, any adverse effect being disguised beneath a cloud of expensive Amouage eau de parfum.

Having welcomed me, he hurried to shut the door, behind which hung his formal black light-weight woollen robe, or *bisht*, edged in gold, which billowed slightly on its hanger in the process. 'Stef'n, my dear, you are always so smart and cool-looking, whereas I am hot. Would you object, O friend, if I removed my *massar* for a moment?' And so he did, revealing a shining bald head with a perfect band of untanned skin above his eyebrows, which did indeed look very much like the top of a boiled egg. This he patted with tissues, plucked from a fretted wooden box on his vast desk using perfectly manicured fingers, before depositing them in the basket by his side. A knock on the door by his coffee-pot wielding assistant saw the *massar* whipped back into place, another cloud of Amouage scented the air, and our meeting resumed its more formal course.

Elsewhere in Arabia, and in Oman's interior, the *kuma* and *massar* are replaced by a loose headscarf ,or *kufiyya*, also called a *ghutrah*, *shamagh* or *sufrah*. This is secured in place by a black *aqal* (egal) – a twisted rope headband – originally used as a camel-hobble. In the Gulf, headcloths tend to be white and worn over a small, crocheted skull cap, or *kufyah*. Each Gulf state wears their white *kufiyya* differently, so that at a trade fair, airport departure lounge or within a massive Dubai megastore, one can tell the Qatari from the Kuwaiti and the Bahraini from the Emirati. Saudi Arabians wear a red-and-white checked *ghutrah*. Elsewhere in Arabia, their colour patterns, such as the Palestinian black-and-white checked version, indicate tribal or national allegiance. So too does the shape of the silver curved dagger, *khunjar*, worn around the waist on a wide belt embroidered with silver thread. These ornate weapons, like their Yemeni counterpart, the *jambiya*, which can be found as far north as Jordan, are often presented as gifts to visiting dignitaries. They were standard issue by fathers to their sons on coming of age, worn with pride once outside the front door on the way to formal occasions such as national day parades in the capital or the most prodigious mosque for Friday prayers in towns throughout Arabia.

The ancient trading town of Sinaw grew at the crossroads of tracks leading to each cardinal point. One ran Northwards to the old capital of Oman, Nizwa. Another ran Southwards towards Masirah and coastal towns on the Arabian Sea, first skirting an outspread fan of wadis which drained into the thirsty plain from the surrounding mountains. Eastwards, tracks hugged the northern limit of the dune fields of the Wahibah Sands and westwards across the oil-bearing plain centred on Fahud before they disappeared into the endless sands of *rub al-khali*. Nomadic *bedu* came here (and still do) to exchange camels and goats for the necessities which were unavailable in the desert: cooking pots, iron tools, and rifles.

There was a time in the early 1990s when I rummaged for treasure in Sinaw's souk, particularly *khunjar* with original blades still intact. Within the cluster of dimly lit and smoke-blackened shops, which smelled strongly of tobacco and frankincense, stood old chests filled with nails, battered coffee pots, camel-hide conical shields and rifle cartridges in distinctly dubious condition. White-eyed visitors there were quite rare in those days, and I was an object of some friendly curiosity as I trawled through the souk. Coffee was offered and conversations started, broken off suddenly to drag me by the hand to the stall where my treasure was most likely to be found. I was watched with feigned indifference by young *bedu* men with their nineteenth-century Martini-Henry breech-loading rifles slung nonchalantly over the shoulders of their not-so-clean *dashadeesh*, the delightful-sounding plural of *dishdasha*.

Women fixed me from the shadows. They wore long black hooded cloaks, or *abbaya*, over loose gowns and pantaloons, the former decorated at the neck and wrists with silver-and-gold needlework. Their wrists and sometimes ankles were banded with heavy beaten-silver bracelets, their faces obscured by beak-like canvas masks or *battoola*. The mask, the generic name for which is *burqa*, covered the forehead to the chin. Their young daughters, by contrast, were unmasked and smiled brilliantly at me, wearing intricate golden tracery headdresses (*harf*) supporting a pendant down the forehead. Westerners like me should avoid looking directly at females. The women in Sinaw's souk were unencumbered by such conventions. Piercing stares from their masked kohl-blackened eyes studied me with curiosity for the weird stranger that I was.

In my experience, Westerners, unless they have been nationalised, are discouraged from wearing regional dress including a *kuma* or *dishdasha*. This is seen as a mild discourtesy to their hosts. The exception is veterans from the Arab Legion or Trucial Oman Scouts, who sport their red-and-white checked *shamagh* and *aqal* with deserved pride during the annual Remembrance Day Cenotaph parade in London. I still have my father's *shamagh*, which he wore to work in Jordan seventy years ago. His heavy double-edged thirty-centimetre long curved *jambiya* hangs now above the fireplace in my study. It is framed by two antique brass coffee pots which I found in Sinaw. I remember, as if it were yesterday, him drawing the dagger out of its black leather sheath to show me and my six-year-old twin brother the dark stains on its blade, which he told us were blood. I repeat this story to the children of visiting family and friends and see the same horrified but delighted expression on their faces as my father saw on ours.

CHAPTER 9

ز   dhaal
زهب   dhahab

Gold

As I have mentioned previously, courtesy is the mark of so many Arabs. One exemplar of that virtue was a career diplomat who served as the director of the Ruler's office in Fujairah during my five Dubai-based years as Regional Naval Officer Gulf, based in the British Consulate in Dubai (the Embassy is in Abu Dhabi). On many occasions he set aside his demanding agenda to make me feel as if I were the only person who mattered in his teeming world. He never looked at the clock or answered the constantly buzzing mobile phone he kept secreted deep in the pocket of his immaculate *bisht* but diverted his full attention to a tall naval officer who had expressed such an interest in the Emirate he administered. I told him that I had just come from a gold factory in the industrial estate which formed part of Fujairah's free port. Having enquired after its owner (a cousin of his, a young entrepreneurial and equally charming *shaykh*), he asked with a twinkle in his eye whether his relative had given me a sample, 'Alas, no, sir,' I replied, 'but at least he did not ask me to remove my shoes and socks and rinse my feet in the trough on the way out designed to capture flecks of gold which might have adhered to the soles of my feet.'

'*mumtaza* (Excellent),' he replied, '*inshallah* ("hopefully" – literally "God willing") they are now an integral part of my carpet!'

It is said that if the estimated total of 171 tons of gold on earth were accumulated, it would form a cube measuring twenty by twenty metres. Other reports have stated that about fifty thousand tonnes of gold remain to be mined, mostly by China, Russia, and Australia, which together extract about one thousand tonnes annually – so just fifty odd years to go then! Gold can be found too in Arabia. Agatharchides of Cnidus, in his much quoted *On the Erythraean Sea*, reported that 'a river runs through the middle of the country [Arabia] which carries down so many nuggets of gold that the silt which is deposited at its mouth gleams'. In the tenth century BCE, gold was reportedly mined at Ophir. It was here that Solomon's 'Ships of Tarshish' called on their return passage from India en route to the head of the Red Sea via the port of Ocelis on the Yemeni coast just north of *bab el-mandeb*. Thesiger thought that Ophir might be in Dhofar region, but a mid-1970s survey considered it to be at *mahd adh-dhahab* (Cradle of Gold) near Medina in Saudi Arabia. This was on the trade route which ran northwards from Aden, where a million tonnes of waste rock was found to contain faint traces of a commodity much prized by the wives of Arabs and others today. There are gold outlets in nearly every souk in Arabia, some of it fashioned into the extravagant and none-too-subtle ornaments produced by dozens of bare-footed Pakistani craftsmen in that Fujairahan factory mentioned above.

One gold extraction process, 'placer' mining, uses mercury to form an amalgam with small particles of gold which can then be processed more readily. I thought my luck was in, because the Omani company which I managed in the mid-2000s owned 258 kilograms of mercury worth about US$8,000 in the year we obtained it. It came from the reservoir below the heavy glass optic of Didamar Lighthouse in the Strait of Hormuz upon which it floated to give the lantern a level and practically frictionless bearing. The obsolete lantern required replacement, so the highly toxic and very heavy liquid mercury needed to be drained off properly into small containers to be shipped safely by sea to our headquarters in Musqat. In early Victorian England, mercury was used in the production of felt used to fashion the headwear of gentlemen. Too much exposure to mercury vapour was said to cause insanity – hence the 'Mad Hatter' in *Alice in Wonderland*. Other derivations are available, but what is certain is that mercury was and is very difficult to transport. We had a buyer for it in the United States. We had the boxed mercury but getting it to the States proved impossible. It resides in a warehouse on the outskirts of Musqat to this day, waiting for another entrepreneur to realise its value.

Musqat used to be a centre for the gold trade. The seventeenth-century English traveller, Dr Fryer, noted (according to Lorimer) that the capital 'was much frequented by merchants who pay gold for Indian commodities. They are treacherous people, gaining as much by fraud as by merchandise'. This was certainly not the case in my time, but perhaps he failed to haggle! Ancient Oman, together with neighbouring UAE, was called Magan. This region was famous for another valuable commodity, copper (*nahas* in Arabic), having been smelted there for centuries by a complex society of miners living in the river valleys of the Al-Hajar mountains. One such valley was the strategic *wadi jizzi*, home to the *julanda* tribe, the approach to which was guarded by the thirteenth-century fort of *hawrah bargha*, perched on a conspicuous 200-metre-high hill above the *wadi* floor. I scrambled up the scree-scattered slope to this remarkable stronghold and marvelled at the complex hydraulic installation which fed the rock-hewn cisterns within its walls necessary to provide it and the surrounding areas with water.

Solomon's slaves were said to excavate copper on the banks of the Red Sea. Both gold and copper were carried northwards to the port of Ezion-Geber at the head of the Gulf of Aqaba where, according to the Bible, King Solomon 'made a navy of ships'. From there it joined the trade routes to and from Memphis, Gaza and Damascus. Camel caravans then ran northwards through Canaan to Asia Minor. This was the land crossed in the late sixteenth century by Englishman Ralph Fitch, who travelled with three fellow merchant adventurers from London to Syria by sea then overland and down the Euphrates to Basra and onwards to Hormuz. He was one of the first Westerners to record evidence of an example of Arabia's most valued geological treasure – black gold.

Bitumen from the Dead Sea had historically been used both to caulk vessels and, appropriately, embalm the dead. In 1583,

Fitch found a lake of bitumen 'that doth continually throwe foorth against the ayre boyling pitch with a filthy smoke' issuing from a fissure in the ground which the Moores [sic – Arabs] called 'the mouth of hell'. He observed that the Arabs 'doe pitch their boates' with bitumen 'so that no water doth enter them'. Little could he realise how much the product spouting from that mouth of hell would transform regional and world history. There are hundreds of detailed accounts of the discovery of oil in Arabia, and I will leave serious study of them to others. However we know that oil was discovered in Persia in 1901 and that Britain's oil interests in Kuwait were guaranteed by a treaty of 1913. Britain's protégé Gulf States signed oil exploration concessions limiting them to British nominated companies. Bahrain and Qatar acquiesced in 1914 and 1916 respectively, with the Trucial sheikhdoms signing in 1922 when British control of the Gulf was complete. No agreement could be signed with Oman because interior/coastal tribal rivalries had resulted in the country being divided in 1920 into the Sultan in Musqat and 'The peoples of Oman' elsewhere under the spiritual leader of the Imam.

In 1932 the first major oil strike in the Gulf was made in Bahrain. A year later another was discovered in the Hejaz, and European and American oil combinations approached Ibn Saud for concessions. If properly exploited, he would no longer need to rely on the tribal taxes of allegiance. Control of the oil fields supplanted his earlier interests in dominating Transjordan. Oil concessions in Qatar were the catalyst for further Anglo/Saudi border disputes, much to the advantage of the United States, whose lawyers later negotiated the formation in 1933 of the company which officially became the Saudi Arabian American Oil Company (Saudi ARAMCO) in 1988. Oil exports started from Oman as late as 1967, however plans to improve the infrastructure of that country were frustrated by the Sultan's very conservative and isolationist attitude. It was reunified as the 'Sultanate of Oman' under Sayyid Sultan Qaboos Al Said, whose cousin I twice served. He is now Oman's deputy prime minister for defence.

Under the terms of the 1982 United Nations Law of the Sea, Iraq is a designated 'geographically disadvantaged' state. Before it was blocked by sunken shipping during the Iran–Iraq war, its principal oil export terminal at Basra was sixty miles up the narrow Shatt al-Arab waterway. As a former Kuwaiti minister once told me, 'Iraq is a big garage with a very little door.' With the waterway unnavigable and massive debt repayments incurred during the war with Iran, much of which went to service Kuwaiti-backed loans, Saddam Hussein wanted improved access to the northern Gulf via Khawr Az-Zubayr and Khawr Abdullah. With envious eyes on the Rumaila oilfield, which was shared with Kuwait, 350 tanks crossed the border on 2 August 1990 and overran Kuwait in three days. ARAMCO and Gulf State oil reserves were under threat and international condemnation was swift and uncompromising. A multi-national force totalling some 750,000 personnel (including, briefly, me) from thirty-one nations was assembled. There was no such coordinated international outrage in 1982 when Argentina invaded the Falklands nor when Iraq had invaded Iran ten years earlier. This fact was not lost on many young Sunni Arabs in the region who admired Saddam Hussein as a strong leader in the mould of Egypt's Gamal Nasser. In December 1990, the month before I arrived in Oman, British citizens were spat at in Musqat's Muttrah souq. The Iraqi casualty bill after Operation DESERT STORM was some 200,000, the majority of which came from the ill-equipped *shi'ite* conscript army from southern Iraq, whose short-lived 1992 resistance after the war Saddam brutally supressed.

One less well-remembered consequence of the war was the fate of thousands of Palestinian guest workers in Kuwait who had no option but to remain because their leader, Yasser Arafat, had backed Saddam. With over 600 oil wells burning in the desert and the northern Gulf choked with crude oil from vandalised pipelines, these unfortunate souls received the brunt of Kuwaiti anger. One of them was the taxi driver who guided us so courteously during the Jordanian trip mentioned at the opening of Chapter 3. Having lost most of his possessions when he was evicted unceremoniously from Kuwait City, he might have looked enviously at golden jewellery, copper ornaments and gas-guzzling supercars, but such was his dignified demeanour, I doubt that he did.

CHAPTER 10

ر   raa'
راس   raas

Head

The sixteenth-century explorer, entitled the 'Great Afonso Dalbuquerque' in his 'Commentaries', considered Arabia to be a 'very small country' called 'the Island of Arabia, because the Persian Sea turns inwards opposite to the Red Sea in such a manner that the country is circular and is almost surrounded by water'. He was mistaken. The area of this 'rough parallelogram' of land, as T. E. Lawrence called it, is within 1.5% of the size of India. Its limits are bounded by a number of headlands (*raas* – the same word as for 'head') which, when transliterated into geographical terms, become Ra's, that apostrophe denoting the glottal stop after the letter *alif* (ا). If we start at Ra's Musandam, which marks the entrance to the Gulf, and move anti-clockwise across the stretch of land which joins Kuwait to Jordan, we encounter Ra's Muhamad and Ra's al Aswad (Black Head) in the Red Sea, Ra's Fartak and Ra's al Madrakah along the Arabian Sea coast and then to its most easterly point, Ra's al Hadd. The tenth-century Persian historian Istakhri wrote a book called *The Limits of the Earth – hudud al-'alam*. So Ra's al Hadd means 'the Head of the Limit' or 'End of the Earth'.

It was this cape which Albuquerque's squadron rounded in August 1507. Imagine the astonishment of the barasti-housed villagers as these strange 1,000-tonne forecastled carracks appeared close offshore with fore and main sails filled by the southwest monsoon – the *khareef*. I sailed past this flat headland after the *khareef* season in late 2007 in a chartered landing craft captained by a permanently smiling master from Myanmar. We were carrying a cargo of newly fabricated five-tonne navigational buoys bound for Masirah. A long, low, gentle swell dipped and raised the bow as a large pod of pilot whales kept station abeam. Not so tranquil during the *khareef*, but the change in sea state encountered by any vessel rounding Ra's al Hadd during that rougher season is remarkable and much welcomed by Albuquerque's crew, I have no doubt. The swell disappears almost immediately, and calm water can be found in the haven of the protected *khawr*, which opens just west of the promontory.

The flat spit at Ra's al Hadd was the site of a World War Two air station, its pot-holed tarmac runways still visible on Google Earth. A civil airport opened thirty kilometres south of it in 2018 to serve the Abu Dhabian gentry who have built villas there and tourists who hope to witness greenback turtles hatching at the Ra's al-Jinz reserve. Before the road barrier and newly built 'blacktop' highway were constructed at the end of the last century, I used to take my children there to prostrate ourselves at sunset behind the confused mounds of earlier nests to witness the first turtles hauling themselves laboriously up the sand then later to carry confused baby turtles back to the sea from our campsite under the stars. Next morning we would explore the adjacent site of a Bronze Age harbour, where ceramics from the Indus Valley had been uncovered together with traces of bitumen-covered third-millennium BCE boats – a clear indication of the ancient maritime trading route to India.

Six kilometres (3 NM) west of Ra's al Hadd lies the extensive but shallow sheltered lagoon of Khawr al-Jaramah. This was used by anti-U-boat Short Sunderland flying boats during World War Two and occasionally as one of the stops for the twenty-seat Imperial Airways flying boat service to India and Australia, typically carrying businessmen or colonial administrators. It is connected to the sea via a narrow tortuous channel which we had navigated sixteen years before my passage to Masirah in a catamaran built from scratch by a close colleague. Four years later the lagoon and its narrows were surveyed by a joint hydrographic team from the Royal Navies of Britain and Oman, which coordinated geodetic stations on the Portuguese fort guarding the *khawr* and which were accommodated, much to the delight of a number of the younger villagers of both sexes, in one of the local shaykh's compacted sand-and-shell shacks. He was sadly blind but very canny and drove a hard bargain for an agreed rent. After this negotiation, he offered us *qahwa* and dates before asking one of his sons to serve us a bowl of *halwa*, a gelatinous sweet confectionery containing dried fruit and nuts and flavoured with rosewater. This is scooped up using the index and middle fingers of one's right hand and then popped into one's mouth with appropriate noises of approval. But to a young sub-lieutenant from the British contingent, this proved to be a sweet too far. It was only with the greatest difficulty and hissed encouragement from his neighbour that he managed to swallow it without gagging. Welcome to Oman, young man!

The surveys of Arabian waters such as those I participated in from 1972 onwards, including this large-scale survey of Khawr al-Jaramah, contributed significantly to a proper understanding of the seas and oceans which bound that 'rough parallelogram' the size of India. Albuquerque's limited geographical knowledge of that 'very small country' was based in part on the earliest maps printed in the later fifteenth century. These were based on information collected by the great Egyptian mathematician and astronomer, Claudius Ptolemaeus, some thirteen hundred years earlier, whose cartographic work lay hidden for over a thousand years until unearthed in Constantinople in 1400 CE. The earliest maps such as the 1478 'Sexta Asiae Tabula' depicted a boot-shaped land bordered to the north by a chain of mountains, Montana Arabiae Felicis, with a city, *Omanum Emporia*, at its heart. A great island-filled rectangular sea, the *Sinus Persicus*, lay to its east and could only be entered via *Asabon Promontorium* – Ra's Musandam. The ancient southern coastal towns of *Ocelis*, *Arabia Emporium*, *Cana Emporium* and *Moscha Portus* were marked, as were *Armuza* and *Gerra* within the Gulf itself. These maps and their subsequent revisions were so diagrammatic that with one subsequently ignored exception, the dominant thumb-shaped peninsula of Qatar was not represented accurately for a further three hundred years until charted by *HMS Scorpion* in 1807.

Arabia's position on the maritime and overland trading routes enabled men of real intellectual ability and foresight, such as Ptolemy, to interact with many cultures and preserve, extract, and enhance the knowledge gained thereby. For example, Yaqub bin Ishaq al-Kindi, whom Bertrand Russell considered to be the only Arabian philosopher of note, had come into contact with Hellenistic, Persian, and Indian science and philosophy. After the Arabian Conquests, the intelligentsia among the Islamic victors were fascinated by the remnants of the ancient civilisations which they encountered. They mined this motherload of knowledge with remarkable skill and perspicacity. The language of the Quran was used to create *adab* – literature. This word comes from the Arabic verb 'to give a banquet', leading to a sense of being cultured or refined. Christian scholars within the Islamic world were contracted to translate ancient scientific and philosophical texts from their original languages into Arabic. These were then absorbed, discussed, and revitalised to be exported later via the Mediterranean Islands and Spain to a Western civilisation which was just emerging from the nadir of its Dark Age.

Russell saw this diligent preservation and enhancement of Greek and Eastern knowledge, including paper manufacture, as the great intellectual legacy of the Arab world without which, he noted, 'the men of the Renaissance might not have suspected how much was to be gained by the revival of classical learning'. The Islamic intelligentsia became vital transmitters of subjects including mathematics, medicine, chemistry, astronomy, and navigation. Our own language is implanted from A to Z with Arabic-derived scientific words, such as alchemy (hence [*al* – the] chemist; chemistry), algebra, algorithm, alkali, almanac, amalgam, azimuth, zenith, and zero. Euclid's textbook on geometry, *Elements*, written in Alexandria in circa 300 BCE, was translated into Arabic in about 800 CE and enriched Western knowledge after it was subsequently translated into Latin by Abelard of Bath in 1120 CE. The Persian Muhammad ibn Zakariya ar-Razi (circa 865 – 923/932, known as Rhazes by the West) is credited with the diagnoses of smallpox and measles and with discovering the principle of vaccination. His encyclopaedia, *al-hawi* – the *Comprehensive Book* – was published in Latin five times between 1488 and 1542.

Perhaps the most familiar philosopher of the early Islamic world was the Persian child prodigy Abu Ali ibn Sina (980 –1037 CE), known to us as Avicenna. He was born in Bukhara and died, it is said, through a surfeit of wine and sex, twenty years before the Seljuk Turks took Baghdad. His medical encyclopaedia, the *qanun* (*Canon – Principles of Medicine*) was used in Europe until the seventeenth century. Other renowned scholars are Abu Hamid al-Ghazali (1058–1111) and Abu al-Walid bin Ahmad bin Rushd (1126–1198) known respectively to the West as Algazel and Averroes. Russell considered that 'men like Avicenna and Averroes are essentially commentators' but some 500 years after the death of the Prophet their influence had changed the Western world in perpetuity. These extraordinary men had used their heads to bequeath a spiritual and cultural legacy of astonishing proportions.

But the legacy of these intellectuals was not always as benevolent to the West. Towards the end of the eighteenth century, followers of Shaykh Muhammed ibn Abdul Wahhab, known as al-*wa'h'abi*, had developed a puritanical and uncompromising dogma based on an undeviating return to the precise rules set out in the Holy Quran. Nothing was permissible which was not covered by the collected sayings of the Prophet and his companions, known as *al-ḥadith*. They formed an allegiance with Mohammed ibn Saud. He was the great-great-grandson of Ibn Saud, whom we met in Chapter 6, the self-proclaimed leader of all *bedu* and their rightful spiritual leader or *imam*. He harboured intentions of dominating the Arabian Peninsula, thereby gaining wealth and influence by the payment of tribal tribute and control of the Holy Cities. Under his direction, the *wa'h'abi* swept out of the Nejd desert and into the Hejaz with the remit to kill every male they encountered in battle, man or boy. No quarter was asked or given, since every *wa'h'abi* killed in conflict was assured a place in paradise. A tribe which embraced wholly this doctrine resided between the coast at Al-Ashkarah, eighty-five kilometres to the south-south-east of Ra's al Hadd and their stronghold thirty kilometres inland.

Another twenty kilometres to the west of Khawr al-Jaramah lies the coastal fishing and shipbuilding town of Sur, which features in Chapter 12. It also featured prominently in an early nineteenth-century conflict between the Sultan of Oman, newly backed by the British, and a recalcitrant tribe, *bani bu-ali*, who had embraced both Wahhabism and local piracy and hated the Christian Europeans. Early attempts to reason with them had been met with a brutal response such that the government in India judged that 'if Britain's newly won prestige among the Arabs were to be preserved' they had 'better retaliate with promptitude and vigour[3]'. In November 1820, a combined Omani–British expedition of some 2,000 men, supported by sixty camels and 300 draught animals to tow the artillery pieces, assembled at Sur. This force advanced overland towards their target to reason with, but if that failed, subdue their adversary. The *bani bu-ali* comprised some 900 fighting men based around their fort, which was defended by eight small-calibre guns. The *wa'h'abi* surprise attack on the unfortunate task force was successful, and as the official British report noted, 'No less than 317 others out of a total of just over 400 had been killed.' The Sultan's force lost about the same number, and the routed army retreated to Musqat 'in case the passes [through the coastal hills] towards Sur had been occupied'.

When the government in India learnt of this defeat, they recognised that support for their new ally, the Sultan (who had taken part and been wounded in the expedition), was 'indispensable for maintaining the advantages of our successes in the Gulph'. It therefore equipped a second and much larger punitive

---

3 All quotations have been taken from a typed report of 'The Expeditions Against the Bani Bu Ali' in my possession. Its date and authorship are not shown in the report.

expedition to 'suppress this little tribe of less than a thousand fighting men'. The task force, loaded into fifteen transports with its horses in eleven native vessels assembled in the anchorage off Sur in mid-January 1821. The *bani bu-ali* had anticipated their arrival. On 10 February, led by their principal *shaykh* Muhammad bin Ali, a select body of their best fighters crept up under cover of darkness, swept aside the pickets, and before the alarm could be raised, 'cut down the troops as they ran from their tents and spearing them through the canvas' before being driven off. Their main weapon, the razor-edged sword, was virtually unchanged since it had been wielded against the Quraysh eleven centuries earlier (Chapter 6).

The British learnt another salutary lesson from dealing with a determined but smaller Arab opposition, but numbers prevailed. In early March a force of 2,700 troops, twelve-pounder cannon and heavy siege guns manned by naval ratings (a precursor to the Siege of Ladysmith at the end of the century) marched through the barren country towards their goal. The latter stages were through the November battle ground where 'numerous half-decayed bodies, skeletons and small shreds of cloth testified this to have been the spot'. But the outcome this time was never in doubt. The *bani bu-ali* fort was surrounded. Just as he was about to order the final assault, the major-general in command cancelled it 'when the shrieks of the women induced me to offer quarter'. Muhammad bin Ali, 'with unruffled dignity' and his arm in a sling from an injury sustained at Sur, came forward to surrender his sword. The walls of his Al-Hamuda fort, which tourists can visit today, were razed to the ground, but he saved his tribe, albeit depleted by some 500 casualties. It is reported that their women folk showed no sign of grief, and in the late afternoon, the remaining tribesmen, 'heads bowed in a humility they disdained to show their conquerors' formed into orderly ranks for the sunset prayer, 'remote in spirit and seemingly unaware of the destruction around them. Such is the Arab character, even that close to the 'End of the Earth' which surely it must have seemed to them at the time.

CHAPTER 11

ز   zaa'
زوجة   zawja

Wife

When I was appointed to Oman towards the end of the first Gulf War in 1991, I was a divorcee with three young children and no intention of changing that wonderfully self-centred status. It was not to last. Three years later I was sitting at the desk in my office in the Sultan's Armed Forces Headquarters, *muaskar al-murtafa'a*. The ma/mu prefix often means 'place', so *muaskar al-murtafa'a* means 'the place of guards (or camp) in the highlands'. My phone rang in the middle of a meeting, and a lady's voice introduced herself as a recently arrived friend of a friend of mine who had given her my number. Being a pompous idiot, I asked her to call me at home later, not knowing that the phone in her flat had yet to be connected. But she did ring again from the phone box across her dusty street later that afternoon. Fortuitously, I told her, there was to be one of Derek Nimmo's 'Whoops there goes my trousers' touring dinner theatre performances, so would she like to join our table, where she might meet some new people? She sensibly said she would.

    Having overcome the instant dislike she had of me, our subsequent friendship blossomed and some months later Annie was a regular guest in my buff-coloured single-storeyed bungalow within the walls of the camp. Security dictated that I would collect her from the small supermarket car park outside the gate and return her there early next morning. My boss, the commander of the Royal Navy of Oman, always first at his desk, called my phone at six thirty in the morning and asked to see me. 'Why are you here so early, Stef'n?' Now, the answer was a little ticklish, as overnight friendly relations between unmarried people were hardly endorsed in that conservative country. But following my father's maxim, 'If in doubt, tell the truth', I explained to His Highness (HH), as such he was, that I had met a lady who had brightened my life. She headed the physiotherapy department at Khoula Hospital and also needed to be at work by 8 a.m., so I would drop her off at her car an hour and a half beforehand then come straight to my desk. He just said, 'Thank you, Stef'n.', and I went back to work.

Twenty-four hours later a brown envelope was dropped onto my desk. In it was a car-pass to the camp, complete with Annie's car registration number and photograph, bearing her name, followed by 'wife of Bennett'. Quite how HH made that happen does not bear too much scrutiny, but the act left me flabbergasted at its efficiency and courtesy and demonstrated that HH at least must have held me in some regard. I proposed to Annie in the airing cupboard in my house in Devon between coming home from Oman in 1997 and being appointed to the consulate in Dubai the following February. She said, 'I'll think about it'! That put me in my place and quite right too, but we arrived in Dubai, very happily married, as 'the Bennetts'. Better than a seconded army couple in Oman, whose first names were Willy and Fanny. They were known to all as 'the Organs'!

Arabic tribal custom has always separated the sexes within the extended household, be it a *bedu* tent, a palm-frond screen (*barasti*) settlement, or a shaykh's palace. The men occupied the *majlis* and the women the *hareem*. While the outside world may be a male-dominated society, behind the front door women often rule, with a strong matriarch very much in charge. Except in the most liberal of families, there is no mixing of the sexes outside the immediate family group. Westerners who are invited to Arabic homes may themselves be segregated, and a male guest would never ask after his host's wife, only after *al-a'ilah*, the family in general. If you ask an Arab how many children he has, he will number his son(s) (*walad*) first, then his daughter(s) (*bint*). One may enquire about the former, never the latter; but if one notes how handsome his sons are, be sure to add *"ma sha*

81

allah" (with God's Grace) and perhaps "but not as good-looking as their father!".

Polygamy was the norm pre-Islamic Arabia. It was revealed to Muhammad that a man could only have four wives, 'but if you fear you cannot maintain equality among them, marry one only or any slave-girls you may own. This will make it easier for you to avoid injustice' [surah 4:3]. The status and rights of women are set out clearly in the Quran. Unlike in the West, women do not take their husband's last name on marriage. The dowry was paid directly to the bride, which was then hers by right, part of which could be reserved for her in the event of divorce. A woman could only divorce her husband on certain grounds, such as impotency or mental disorder, however one wise commentor has noted that many women who found their husbands to be intolerable behaved so obstreperously towards him that he was forced to divorce her to save face in front of his relatives!

Annie, who is quite tolerant towards me, is a remarkable woman. A few months after we met, I asked her whether she had ever abseiled. Having reasonably asked, 'Why?', I explained that a group of us wanted to traverse the spectacular *kahf al-hutah* karst limestone cave complex from its entrance at the end of a blind *wadi* near the village of *al-hutah* in the Interior (*dhakhilliyah*) region, through the mountains to its limit near the village of *bani-subh* two and a half kilometres to the south. This was many years before a narrow-gauge railway had been built to take tourists into the caverns at its southern end. In preparation, I set up a rope system from the flat roof of my bungalow, and Annie practised abseiling down the short distance past the kitchen window, much to the surprise of our delightful Indian cook, Da Costa.

The lower caves might now be floodlit, but they certainly flood, and before attempting passage from the upper end, the lower end must first be checked. Access into the lower caverns to check water levels involved a scramble down a slimy near-vertical tunnel in the floor of a huge gaping cave, its interior blocked with rock falls. A dusty one-kilometre hike past stalagmites, one shaped like a lion's head, must be undertaken amid towering yellow-oche columns which mark the entrances to a confusing maze of side passages then onwards down a muddy incline to the main 800-metre-long subterranean fish-filled lake. The fish, having never seen the light of day, are blind, with a membrane over their tiny pink eyes. Fifty metres into this lake, the walls and ceiling close into a gap no more than three metres wide. If the water is up to the roof, one cannot, indeed (unless one has a death wish) must not, attempt the passage from the upper northern end, as there is no way back. Having checked this out the afternoon before, all was well.

Next morning we were driven up a graded track and across the flat-topped quartz-streaked grey limestone mountain to the northern end of the cave system, where the thankfully dry bed of *wadi hutah* turns through ninety degrees into a low cave carved out of the cliff face. In its floor are a number of shiny sink holes burnished by detritus carried forcibly by floods from the last rainfall. This was our abseil entry into the main chamber of *al-kahf al-hutah* – Hooti Cave. And what a chamber it is. Imagine the interior of St Paul's Cathedral, into which a giant has flung a thousand boulders, with countless pink and gold stalactites hanging like organ pipes from its roof. Our powerful torch beams could only just illuminate the highest of them. Breathtakingly beautiful. Then two more long abseils into the darkness below, as the cave turns back on itself twice in a zigzag descent to a series of bathtub-like pools. These lead to a lake, the other end of which we had checked the day before.

Weighed down by our sodden climbing ropes, we made the long, chilly swim across the lake, its surface rippled by the reassuring and warming breeze blowing from the *wadi* mouth some three kilometres behind us. It was reassuring because if there were no breeze, there was no way back! The walls and roof closed in as we found once more the other side of the narrow, low gap at its end, surrounded by the same welcoming fish which nibbled at our fingers. One of Annie's first, but by no means the last, Arabian adventures. Brave lady.

Our four-year stint in Dubai was decorated by memorable diversions such as my flight out in a United States Navy Grumman C2 Greyhound 'COD' aircraft to catch the arrestor wires of the vast floating airfield, which was the *USS John C Stennis*, and being catapulted off again from zero to one hundred and forty knots in just under two seconds. We scoured the fossil fields at the foot of Jebal Qatar for desert roses and watched camels wading up to their bellies in the brackish and mangrove-lined waters of Khawr Kalba in the Emirate of Fujairah, from where we sailed northwards from the border town of Dibba in the two-masted *Charlotte Anne* to re-explore the fiords of the southern Musandam Peninsula.

It was on this trip that we surfaced unawares from snorkelling amid the inquisitive multicoloured tropical fish populating the inshore coral reefs into an oily slick of illegal bilge washings from a tanker in the bunkering anchorage off Khawr Fakkan. It took the entire contents of a litre-bottle of detergent to dissolve the oil and tar from our matted hair and streaked-brown bodies. We flew peregrine and saker falcons (from the Arabic *saqr* – 'falcon') from padded gloves at dawn in the rose-red dunes of the Al-Maha (Arabian Oryx) resort and witnessed the victorious Frankie Dettori springing from his saddle at the world's richest horse race – the Dubai World Cup. But it was not all work; there was some relaxation too. Annie won a raffle prize at the pre-Dubai Classic exhibition golf match at the nine-hole Jebal Ali course presented by a line-up including Thomas Bjorn, Darren Clarke, Mark O'Meara, Colin Montgomery, and Tiger Woods. She kissed them all on the cheeks to a round of envious applause. Tough life in the Gulf.

Parts of the tasks in my final Dubai-based naval appointment which were not directly concerned with pre-planning and keeping abreast of daily operations of deployed royal naval vessels was my regular 'parish round' of Gulf states. I would fly to Riyadh, Kuwait, Qatar, and Bahrain to gauge the reaction and effectiveness of these deployments. Feedback would come from our diplomats and their military attachés but perhaps more importantly from a host of Arabic interlocutors, from officials at airport customs, port management, and ministries to businessmen in construction, infrastructure, and tourism.

Of course it took some time to gain their confidence, but once established I could not go through an airport or port security building on my diplomatic passport without a cry of, 'O, Mr Stef'n, how are you, my dear? Join us,' followed by ubiquitous *qahwa* and dates to gossip and laugh about what was in the local paper or being streamed on Al-Jazirah TV. International politics or why the Royal Navy was in the Gulf never came into it; rather what I took away from these informal meetings was a clearer picture about what they thought of new housing developments, an outrageous hike in utility or fuel costs, the best 4WD to purchase and the incompetency or otherwise of their leaders. They never asked for a favour or offered a 'gift' to facilitate a visa request or assist with some scheme or other. They were just delightful company for that brief encounter and considered me to be their equal in every respect. Annie said I viewed Arabia through rose-tinted glasses. Perhaps I did a little but always while keeping serious matters in sharp focus, unlike those blind fish and the occasional visiting British politician.

CHAPTER 12

س   seen
سفينة   safeena

Ship

Just to the south-east of Oman's capital Musqat, literally the place where the mountains fall into the sea, the dark coast suddenly changes to light flat-topped sandstone hills. Encircled by two crumbling headlands and an offshore island lies the bright turquoise bay of *bandar jissah*. In the early 1980s a Royal Naval warship on a goodwill visit had found an uncharted rock within its sheltered embrace the hard way! It was surveyed under my direction a decade later by a joint British Royal Navy and Royal Navy of Oman team, but thirteen centuries earlier other ships had entered this natural harbour intent on a much less peaceful purpose. An amphibious landing force had been dispatched by Caliph Mu'awiya from his headquarters in Damascus to re-impose suzerainty over the recalcitrant Julanda tribes of Oman who had ceased to pay the annual tax of allegiance – *jizya* – to the Caliphate.

While the hydrographic survey continued, I crossed the nearby curving sand spit at Yitti and followed the ancient track up the long, dry water course of *wadi al-mih* to where it widened into the stone-strewn valley of *sayh hatat* beneath the hot brown mountains of *jebel at-ta'iyyin*. It was here in 680 CE that the two Muslim armies faced each other across the sweltering rock-strewn valley floor. The Omani general, Sayyid (Prince) Sulliman al-Julanda, had the strategic advantage. On his signal the left and right flanks of his forces flowed up either side of the valley and then swept down on the advancing Caliphate army, attacking them from three sides. The Caliphate general was slain where he stood and his forces were annihilated. Only a few were able to flee back down the *wadi* to the shelter of their ships anchored in *bandar jissah*.

But what ships were these and what did they look like? Dhow is not an Arab word, though it came to be accepted as the generic term for all Arabian craft, each of which, like the double-ended *baggarah*, *battil*, and *zaruqah*, had a distinct name. The *boum* is another double-ended vessel of between 75 and 400 tonnes, with a distinct long, straight stem post which juts forward at 45 degrees. The small *sambuq* (20 to 150 tonnes) and its even smaller cousin the *shu'i* (15 tonnes maximum) have low curved scimitar-shaped stern posts and high square-ended sterns introduced after the arrival of the Portuguese in the seventeenth century. These were the pearling vessels of the Gulf.

All these vessels were generally of carvel construction in which hand-sawn side planks are all flush, the edges laid close and caulked with coir braids soaked in fish oil. Vessels were fitted with teak or coconut wood spars and *daql* (masts – literally 'palm trunk'). Sails were woven originally from date or coconut palm leaf fibre but were replaced in later centuries with cotton cloth. The word 'cotton' comes from the Arabic *qutun*, as does the name for the after-most mast, the mizzen. The Arab lateen (or settee) sail had a short luff at its forward end making it four-sided. It produced an effective fore and aft rig for sailing closer to the wind and could be trimmed thwartships for running before it. The vessels were steered with a stern oar, stern rudders being a later twelfth- or thirteenth-century innovation.

After the cedar and juniper forests had been reduced to small inaccessible groves like those found on the 'Asir range in Yemen and the Sayq plateau in Oman, hardwoods, particularly teak (*saf*) from India and mangrove poles from East Africa had to be exported to meet the demands of both urban and maritime construction needs. Coconut wood came from Indian Ocean islands like the Maldives, husks being beaten to produce the coir fibre with which the planks were sewn together and caulked. Stitching techniques may have been developed in the construction of Sumerian reed boats and exported throughout Arabia by early mariners. The scarcity of Arabian iron ore, and the cost of smelting and fashioning it into nails without a ready supply of charcoal, made the use of plentiful coir twine the most cost-effective ship construction solution for vessels with easily beached rounded hulls. Their sailing seasons avoided periods of heavy weather thereby removing the requirement to contend with violent seas.

Greco-Roman vessels were more seaworthy than their Arab/Persian counterparts because they were nailed together rather than being sewn and could fare better during the stronger south-west monsoon (*khareef*) season. In these closed season months, vessels were beached and repaired at specialist centres, such as Umm al Qaiwain, Bahrain, Kuwait, or Sur, where tidal creeks permitted large vessels to be both constructed and refitted. However these sleek but lightly built vessels were no match for the sturdy, high-sided and heavily armed carracks in which European explorers, adventurers, and invaders like Albuquerque arrived in Arabian waters from the late fifteenth century onwards. These were square-rigged on the fore and main and lateen-rigged on the mizzen. They were superseded by the more efficient galleon during the seventeenth century. This eliminated the high fore-castle, which made the vessels more manoeuvrable and enabled them to sail closer to the wind.

Other types of vessel saw action in Arabian waters. In the late fifteenth century, the last Mamluk Sultan of Egypt, spurred on by Venice, which relied on spice supply via the Red Sea, despatched a fleet of galleys through the Bab al Mandeb to seek out and destroy Portuguese vessels in the Arabian Sea. These were propelled by a square sail on the foremast and a large lateen sail on the main. Sails were used for passage but were struck before battle. Propulsion in action was obtained from a single bank or oars. The ram had given way to canon, but these could only be mounted to fire forward. Their only advantage was manoeuvrability in battle. Superior Portuguese gunnery reduced the Mamluk fleet to matchwood.

The armed merchantmen of the Honourable East India Company, called 'East Indiamen', and their Dutch counterparts were purpose-built monarchs of the sea. The former were built in the company's own dockyard at Deptford and later in their shipyards in Mumbai (Bombay), which the Arabs called Colobah. These vessels were decorated with fine carving and were both luxurious and well-armed, the so-called aristocrats of the shipping world. Other less noble mariners also frequented Arabian waters.

The Arab word for 'pirate' is *korsan* and like terrestrial raiding by the *bedu*, early Arab sailors were not averse to maritime raiding. In 637 CE a piratical raiding force sailed from the Omani ports of Sohar and Musqat to 'ravage the rich and prosperous dominions of the idolatrous Hindoos' returning, so the early twentieth-century diplomat Colonel S. B. Miles tells us, 'with a splendid booty'. The present and highly intelligent Emir of Sharjah, upon whom I called several times during my time in Dubai, succeeded his assassinated brother in 1972. He survived a coup attempt by his elder brother in 1975 and is, as of 2023, the longest reigning Arab ruler. He published his doctorate thesis from the University of Exeter in 1986 on 'The Myth of Arab Piracy in the Gulf'. This thesis proposed that the account by the renowned historian and colonial administrator J. G. Lorimer contained deliberate misrepresentations of the history of the Arabian Peninsula. It, according to the author, 'was able to present falsehoods and rumours as irrefutable facts'. He refuted the statement that 'over the centuries the tribes of the southern shore of the Gulf had acquired notoriety as pirates', stating that 'the Gulf was always a peaceful waterway that served more as a connecting link between the peoples living on its shores than a divider; and with the exception of Rahma bin Jabir, pirates were not known in the Gulf'.

This is not the place to argue for or against Shaykh Sultan's convictions, but he was right to mention the late eighteenth-century Qatar-based Rahmah bin Jabir al-Jalhami, described by an English traveller as 'the most successful and most generally tolerated pirate, perhaps, that ever infested any sea'. He was covered in battle scars, sported an eyepatch and cheekily called his flagship *Al-Manowar* ('Man of War'). Captain Haines Indian

Navy reported that pirate vessels belonging to an ambitious and avaricious Dhofar-based Arab merchant, 'united with a predilection for a roving life' captured an American ship in the Red Sea and murdered all the crew with the exception of one boy who was brought back to Raysut and 'educated in the tenets of the Mohammedan faith'. When Haines met him in 1835, 'he had nearly forgotten his mother tongue, but had a wife and several children, and seemed perfectly contented with his lot.

I met such a man in Ra's al-Khaimah. He had not been kidnapped but had jumped ship as a youthful crewmember of a visiting merchant navy vessel in the late 1950s. He also had a wife and several children and became, much to my astonishment, a musician with the ruler's military band, which played on the quayside when Royal Navy ships made their annual courtesy call. I met him during the first of several visits to Ra's al Khaimah, when he engaged me with a huge smile of yellow teeth and a broad Geordie accent. He just wanted to make certain that I would not 'shop' him. Being so reassured, he played tunefully throughout the rest of my time in the Gulf.

Miles commented that European pirates, whose 'reckless captains created a terrible sensation', eclipsed 'the hole-and-corner business' of native piracy. Instead of 'small boats from Malabar and Sind[h], there were now Indian Seas vessels with tiers of guns and manned by the first seamen of Europe'. These pirates, including those from Daibul on India's West Coast based in Socotra (named 'Cacotoia' on a Viennese map of 1522), targeted the Red and Arabian Seas and the Indian Ocean from the late seventeenth century. The brutal thug, John Avery, alias Long Ben, operated from a base in Madagascar. The American Captain Tew and his French ally, M. Misson, found rich pickings in the Gulf of Aden during their voyages. There was some comeuppance, as both died during their depredations. The debaucheries of Western pirates were appalling and not in the least romantic. Pity the poor slaves and Mecca-bound pilgrims who had the misfortune to encounter them. Captain Kidd, operating initially under a letter of marque to act against pirates, based himself at Aden for a while. Not averse to a little piracy himself, he captured the Indian-owned and richly laden *Quedagh Merchant*. He would later have to answer for this and other transgressions. After his execution in 1701, the sale of Kidd's effects fittingly bought the land on which now stands the National Maritime Museum at Greenwich.

Maritime accidents are no respecters of life either, but some are luckier than others. In 1684, the *Merchant's Delight* from London was wrecked on the fringing reefs of Masirah Island. In Lorimer's account, the local *bedu*, having been promised a half-share of the salvaged cargo, 'treated the crew with unexpected kindness' and conveyed them with the rest of the cargo to Musqat. This was in contrast to the fate of seventeen of the crew of a lifeboat from *SS Baron Innerdale*, who in 1904, with the exception of a boy passenger, were massacred to a man. The Sultan of Oman, Faisal, visited the island to investigate. The perpetrators were executed and the shaykh was banished from the island. I often visited Masirah on both business and pleasure. On the last day of 2006 we observed a minute's silence by the monument to this massacre (which incorrectly names the ship as *Baron Inverdale*), standing amid the rocks just above our camp with just friends and flamingos for company.

The word 'Persia' applies to the province of Pars (Fars in Arabic), which gave Persia's language its name. Iran only acquired its formal name in 1935, however the inhabitants of Persia have always referred to their country as Iran, from *aryanam* – 'the land of the Aryans'. Wooden-walled warships from rival Christian nations routinely tested their respective maritime capabilities off the Persian coast from the early seventeenth century onwards. One such encounter occurred in 1620 off Jask to the south of the Strait of Hormuz. A combined Dutch and Portuguese taskforce engaged a numerically inferior English squadron comprising *London* (800 tonnes), *Hart* (500 tonnes), and *Roebuck* (300 tonnes), which demonstrated, and not for the first or last time, the superiority of English gunnery.

The Dutch and Portuguese retired to Hormuz to repair damaged rigging, having committed the body of their vice admiral to the deep embrace of the Gulf of Oman. *HMS Roebuck* was the ship in which William Dampier made a voyage of discovery around Australia between 1699 and 1701. I was fortunate to be appointed in command of the brand-new *HMS Roebuck*, then the world's most advanced hydrographic survey ship, almost three hundred years later. My time in command included the definitive survey of the waters off Gibraltar, where Tariq ibn Ziyad had started his invasion of Hispania in the early eighth century and had the 'Rock' named after him – *jebal tar[iq]*. Two years after I had left the Royal Navy, *Roebuck* played a distinguished role as part of the 2003 taskforce sent to overthrow Saddam Hussein in the second Gulf War.

The three seventeenth-century Royal Naval ships lay up at Sur during the summer of 1612, where local shipbuilders had already been influenced considerably by the nailed and transom-sterned construction of Portuguese galleons. *Roebuck* and her sister ships were yet another advance in shipbuilding techniques. These skills, adopted by Omani artisans at Sur, were later maximised by Sultan bin Saif al-Ya'ribi, the 'liberator' of Musqat (Chapter 13), who ordered captured Portuguese ships to be stripped down and analysed. The transom stern was combined with a two-masted lateen rig to form a fleet of well-armed *sumbuq*, which in time gave rise to a new class of high-sterned vessels, the precursor to the larger and more elaborate *baghlah* and *ghanjah* vessels. The 150- to 500-tonne *baghlah* was both square and lateen rigged and did not emerge as a distinctive class until the nineteenth century. It had a high poop deck and quarter galleys, and its transom stern was often carved elaborately. Larger vessels stepped three masts. The class was crossbred from East Indiamen and adapted by Omani craftsmen. The *ghanjah* was a derivation of the *baghlah* and was distinguished by a curved stem head with a trefoil crest. By the end of the seventeenth century, Oman had created a fleet to rival any other in Arabian waters. It was said that any of its ships could sail round the clumsy merchantmen that hailed from the Thames. They were not always so dominant. A naval engagement off Ra's al

Hadd in 1698 between two Portuguese frigates and eight Omani *sambuq* resulted in the destruction of the Omani flotilla and the death of its commander, the *wali* (governor) of Muttrah.

Arab crews also manned the fleets of potential rivals, but as always, their employer had to command loyalty. The brutal eighteenth-century Persian ruler, Nadir Shah, whose 'military prowess' Lorimer noted 'was greater than his political acumen', as no such man. Arab crews manning three of his ships mutinied in August 1740, murdered the Persian admiral and then sailed for their former bases at Qeshm and Ra's al Khaimah. A flotilla under the command of the newly appointed Persian admiral, 'who had never seen the sea or a ship in his life', briefly engaged with their rivals, but soon returned to Bandar 'Abbas on the orders of the terrified admiral, pursued by the mutineers manning their superior *sambuq*.

I have spent hours sitting at Sur, under the barasti shade coverings of a half-formed *boum*, *sambuq* or *shu'i*, watching Arab craftsmen rummaging among the heaps of indigenous *qarat* and *sidr* (species of acacia) for the perfect crook from which to fashion the knee or ribs of a growing vessel. I would sit fascinated as two old seafarers coordinated the application of *zayt samak* (fish oil) to the teak plants by alternately chanting the lines of an ancient sea shanty, one inside, one outside the half-finished hull. Before I left, I was encouraged to pick up one of the old iron nails which superseded sewn construction in the nineteenth century and take it home with me, for a nail which has sailed countless times through the seven seas and returned home in safety was considered, like the mariners it secured, to be lucky. One such nail sits in front of me as I write this today.

CHAPTER 13

ش   sheen
شمال   shamaal

North Wind

The Arabic for north is *shamaal*. The southern waters of the Gulf had originally been called 'the Shemal Region' from the same name given to the north-westerly winds generated by weather fronts over Iran and Iraq. These strong three- to five-day force 8 (38 knot/70 kilometres per hour (k/hr)) winds drove the sand dunes southwards and hindered Byzantine square-rigged vessels from passing Ra's Musandam because of their inability to tack effectively into the wind. The strength of the wind sweeps up sand from the deserts of Syria before blasting it out in stinging waves over Iraq and the states bordering the Gulf and its approaches. The generic term for a severe wind is *haboob*, but there are as many local names for winds in Arabia as there are in Europe and elsewhere. A dangerous northerly or westerly wind in the Arabian Sea is called '*belat*', probably derived from *balad* – 'country' – meaning 'off the land'. This is the region most commonly prone to the impact of tropical revolving storms or cyclones (*a'asa'ar*), which are called typhoons in the Pacific from the Arabic word *tuf'aan*, meaning 'flood' or 'deluge'. Cyclones have historically dumped hundreds of thousands of tonnes of rainwater onto the mountains to cascade downwards, carving cliffs and *wadi* beds from the limestone and flooding the plains.

    I witnessed my first Arabian cyclone in 1996. Named '02A', it started in the Gulf of Aden then swung menacingly northwards towards Oman, striking the coast at Ra's Madrakah and inundating the *jiddat harasis*, home to the then protected oryx. Paradoxically, this brought them considerable benefit, as the desert bloomed and quadrupled their normally scant grazing.

Damage was particularly severe in Yemen, where the heaviest rainfall in seventy years was dumped onto the historic town of Marib. It tragically killed over three hundred people as their houses, built on the *wadi* floors, were swept away. However, Cyclone 02A was a comparatively minor event compared to super-cyclonic storm 'Gonu', which struck Oman in June 2007.

As mentioned earlier, I had returned to Oman in early 2005 to manage a new privately owned aids to navigation (AtoN) company. As Chapter 24 recounts, these AtoN included large 5-tonne buoys designed to remain 'on station' in all but the most extreme sea conditions. That is, they should be available to the mariner for between 97% and 99.8% of the time, depending on how important they are to safe navigation. According to strict international standards, a 'vital' Category One AtoN, whether a floating buoy, fixed beacon or lighthouse, must be fully operational for at least 998 days in any 1,000-day period. Put another way, such AtoN can have a maximum downtime of only two days in three years. To achieve this, buoys contain internal watertight compartments to withstand collisions and are secured to a 3-tonne sinker on the seabed by a heavy chain cable. This is typically three times as long as the depth of water in which they float to allow the chain catenary to absorb the violent surges the buoy experiences from wave action. A Force Eight wind in open water will, in time, build up waves measuring three to four metres from crest to trough. The buoys we deployed were designed to cope with waves of up to seven metres – a very high sea state generated by prolonged fifty-knot storm force 10 winds.

I had experienced such seas many times during my time in the navy, but the Category 5 super cyclone Gonu, which became the strongest ever recorded in the Arabian Sea, had winds peaking at 130 knots (240 k/hr), almost twice that of a storm 10 and way beyond a hurricane. The wave size and force of the wind were expected to exceed considerably the design parameters of our buoys and land-based AtoN. Gonu struck Ra's al Hadd from a blackened sky on 6 June, with winds howling in at 80 knots

(145 k/hr). Steep-sided waves over ten metres tall hurtled towards the shore. We had recently refurbished the steel lattice tower of a fifty-year-old fifty-metre-tall lighthouse at Ra's al Hadd. Would it still be standing the following day, and how many buoys would be wiped from our records?

Gonu, which inflicted over US$4 billion worth of damage, was considered to be Oman's worst recorded natural disaster. Fifty souls sadly lost their lives, a total which would have been significantly higher had it not been for the superb pre-impact plans which the government had enacted before it struck. While it raged outside, we waited in our villa as the horizontal hurricane-driven rain violently rattled our windows, palm fronds whistling by. Ra's al Hadd lighthouse, which we could monitor remotely, shuddered but remained operational throughout. The fate of the buoys was less certain. We had already established a network of AtoN monitors along Oman's 1,800-kilometre coastline (Oman is 3% larger than Italy). Reports started to come in from port authorities and our regional observers, who were rewarded with an appropriate consideration for their services. The principal ports (*mina*) at Salalah, Musqat, the oil export terminal at Mina Fahl (mentioned below) and Sohar reported superficial damage to topmarks but no major AtoN casualties. The only unreported area was to the southeast of Musqat's Mina Sultan Qaboos.

Having first rescued a couple of friends and their thirteen-day-old baby from their flooded villa, I set out next day in my Nissan Patrol Landcruiser to investigate, the filthy soup-thick water occasionally reaching its side windows. Roads and bridges had been washed away. Overflowing *wadi* were still discharging boiling brown floodwater into the sea, filled with splintered tree trunks and the occasional slowly spinning Toyota truck. Parked cars had been concertinaed together in saw-toothed rows. Aluminium car ports were folded up against their houses. A 10-tonne fibreglass boat lay tilted across a shop's entrance, as if it had been tossed their by a disgruntled giant. But to my delighted astonishment, all but one of the coastal buoys were faithfully 'watching', nodding on their moorings in the rapidly decreasing swell. The exception was one which had been laid in a very exposed location. It was miraculously our only maritime casualty. Two days later, my small Omani team, assisted by a chartered tug, recovered a very battered buoy, still attached to its mooring, from a rocky bay, its welded 10-millimetre steel hull ripped open by the sheer force of the waves. Within forty-eight hours the team had installed an emergency replacement to keep mariners safe. This was achieved to the highest standards of seamanship and health and safety by a group of young men whom I had recruited just two years earlier. They had no previous maritime or engineering experience. Such a credit to themselves, their tribes and their nation.

Perhaps I should not have been surprised. It was in their blood. Arab seafarers had sailed these waters since antiquity. Their knowledge of stars and wind patterns far outstripped that of their Western counterparts. Ancient seafarers generally sailed within sight of land, but their oceanic voyages to Africa and the Indian sub-continent relied on a basic knowledge of astronomy. It goes without saying that skills used for ocean navigation were also used in the equally featureless desert, guided at sea as on land by towers of fire (Chapter 24). These ancient mariners also utilised the monsoon winds. It was not until 100 BCE, so *The Periplus of the Erythaean Sea* tells us, that the Roman Empire utilised the phenomena, having been told of this 'discovery' by the Greek Hippalus.

There were three possible sailing periods along the Arabian Sea coast from Ra's al-Hadd to Aden and back. Each was governed by the predicable winds generated by the annual monsoons. The term 'monsoon' comes from the Arabic for season – *mawsim*. The south-west monsoon (*al-khareef*) blows from May to October. Ports such as Raysut (Salalah) and its neighbour, Mirbat, were closed from mid-June to mid-August due to excessive wind and swells. This gave a long late-spring sailing season from the end of March to mid-June and a short late-summer season from August to September for the passage to Ra's al-Hadd and beyond. A benign season for the return journey to Salalah and Aden could be made during the more gentle northeast monsoon (*azyab*), which ran from late-October to March.

By the end of the third millennium BCE, maritime trading routes, as evidenced by that Bronze Age port just south of Ra's al Hadd mentioned in Chapter 10, had been established from Failaka (an island off Kuwait) down through the Gulf to extend eastwards to the Indus valley and as far south as Zanzibar. The lateen-sailed ships plying these routes supplied commodities, including African slaves, to the Sumerian cities in Mesopotamia. An early Akkadian tablet from 2,300 BCE states that ships from Melukhkha (the old name for the Makran coast), Magan (Oman/UAE) and Dilmun (Qatar/Bahrain) were made to tie up at Akkad near modern-day Baghdad. It is said that a series of salt-laden winter *shamaal*, some 100 years after that tablet was inscribed, resulted in major crop failures and famine which precipitated the demise of Akkad and its eponymous empire.

Mesopotamia had an insatiable demand for oriental goods. Wood, spices, and lapis lazuli came from India and passed through Dilmun. Traders used personalised 'Dilmun' seals o identify and protect their goods, relics of which have been found right along the route from the Indus to Iraq. In the first millennium BCE, Arab seafarers formed part of the crews of Solomon's 'Ships of Tarshish', transporting luxuries from India. The voyage, so the Book of Kings tells us, was made 'once in three years', with ships laden with 'gold and silver, ivory and apes, and peacocks'. A thousand years later, these vessels would have rendezvoused with Indian ships at the southern end of the Red Sea at a port they called Ophir. The viability of the two maritime trade routes via the Red Sea or the Gulf depended, then as now, on who controlled the choke points of the Bab al-Mandeb and the Strait of Hormuz. In the eleventh and twelfth centuries CE, both routes pumped African and Eastern cargoes into their respective entrepot: Ormuz (near modern-day Bandar Abbas), Jeddah, and Port Sudan on the opposite side of the Red Sea. Other staging posts on the westward route via the Red Sea were Kana/Cana on the south coast of the Hadhramaut in Yemen, Muza [Hodeida], and Leuke Kome at the head of the Red Sea. Those who governed those ports grew wealthy on customs levies just as the Nabateans had at Petra a thousand years earlier.

The presence of Persian ships carrying silk traders from Siraf halfway up the Iranian Gulf coast can be found in early eighth century CE Chinese records. Arab and Persian vessels would depart from Basra and Siraf after the autumn equinox. They first made for Oman's *al-batinah* coast to store ship at Sohar or Musqat before using the steady winds of the north-east monsoon to reach the Malabar Coast of South-West India in a month and Canton in China by May. Deep in the carvel hulls of their lateen-sailed vessels were packed export cargoes of raw materials such as linen, cotton, wool, and iron ore as well as finished rugs and metalwork. They also later carried that staple of trading, gold bullion, minted from the Arab-controlled mines in Africa. They returned about a year later, utilising the start of the new north-east monsoon season to reach the Dhofar coast in March, laden, as Sindbad's author recounts, with 'great store of diamonds ... cloves and ginger and all manner of spices'. The captains, or *nawkhuda*, of such vessels would then coast northwards at the start of the south-west monsoon, reaching Musqat in the early summer. The round trip from the Gulf to Cochin and back lasted about eighteen months.

By the sixth century CE, just before the Arabian conquests, the coastal border town of Dibah between Oman and the UAE had become a major port. Four hundred years later, the port of Sohar, 45 NM/80 km south-southeast was reported by Persian historian Istakhri to be the 'emporium of the whole world' a 'populous and beautiful spot with houses that are high and built of teak wood and bricks; a hallway to China, the store house of the East and Iraq and the stay of Yemen'. It boasted glass manufacturing, copper smelting, and iron working industries and had its own clay pit and brickworks. Its success was not to last. In 965 CE, two hundred and eight-five years after its drubbing at the hands of Sulliman al-Julanda, it was sacked by a Caliphate taskforce from Basra, and eighty-nine Sohari vessels were reduced to ashes. Three years before William landed at Hastings to conquer England, the southern Persian Sunni Seljuk Turks took control of Ormuz in 1063, and a year later, Seljuk's grandson, Kadir Bay (Kaward – 'The Wolf') invaded and subjugated northern Oman. He who controls the Strait of Hormuz, controls the Gulf, a fact which Iran, Great Britain and the USA recognise to this day.

In the twelfth century CE, a bold tribe, *al-'abd al-qais*, (later named *al-qasimi*) established a strong trading and raiding base on Jazireh-ye Qeys off the Persian coast in the Gulf. They later settled at Ra's al Khaimah. The Arab geographer ,Yaqut (d.1229), noted that 'Qais' had replaced Siraf as 'the stopping place for ships crossing between India and Fars', a position it held for two hundred years. Because of the importance of the alternative Red Sea route, the wealth and status of the Dhofar region grew considerably. This was attested to by the famous North African geographer, Abu Abdullah Muhammed ibn 'Abdullah al-Lawati – Ibn Battuta – who visited Salalah in 1325 and again in 1347. He made no mention of the great cyclone which struck the region in the year of his first visit so clearly must have missed it. On his return from his travels throughout the Islamic Empire, he wrote his masterful account *ar-rihlah (The Journey)*. He had been preceded some thirty-five years earlier by Marco Polo, who noted that 'Dhofar [Salalah] is a great and noble fine city' which 'stands upon the sea and has a very good haven, so that there is great traffic of shipping between this and India' to which he noted are shipped 'great numbers of horses'. The Dhofari rainy monsoon period which preceded the sailing season was ideal for the breeding, care, and improvement of high-quality horseflesh, which was first transported to Qalhat between Ra's al Hadd and Musqat, which Ibn Battuta also visited, as recounted in Chapter 16.

Musqat, with its sheltered khawr, was a natural maritime trading centre. It could be identified from seaward by the steep-sided, red-coloured offshore island with the appearance of a stallion (*fahl*). It still guards Mina Fahl, the large single buoy mooring complex from which Very Large Crude Carriers (VLCC) embark, their valuable cargoes piped in from the interior. Tourist diving companies today mistakenly call *jazirat fahl* 'Shark Island' because its waters are patrolled by hundreds of black-tipped reef sharks (*qirsh*). 'Stallion' is so much better. Musqat and the other coastal trading centres supplied a constant source of experienced seafarers and vessels to navigate the trade routes to India, Serendib (Sri Lanka), Malacca, and East Africa. But with the arrival of the Portuguese and their new maritime artery round the Cape of Good Hope, old trading cities like Qalhat would crumble into dust.

The Portuguese, bringing with them both destruction and new maritime technologies, would be eventually expelled by Sultan bin Saif al-Ya'ribi in the mid-seventeenth century. Musqat flourished again. An English traveller (quoted by Lorimer) noted in 1676 that within the 'fiery bosom of its vast and torrid mountains [that] no shade but heaven does hide ... lay a secure harbour for the pilots of their weather-beaten ships'. In the next bay to the southeast, near where our buoy had been hurled ashore during Cyclone Gonu, lay a small sailing club, which launched its boats down a ramp. There I found, bought and refurbished a forgotten eighteen-foot Drascombe lugger. Quite how it got there from the building yard in Totnes, Devon, I have no idea. My wife preferred our twin-engined powerboat berthed in the adjacent modern marina, but *Mahala*, with its lone Englishman at the helm, was a regular Friday feature off Musqat's indented coastline. The onshore breeze, harnessed by its three dark-red sails, kept me entirely content, except of course when a *shamaal* arrived to spoil such memorable Arabian afternoons.

CHAPTER 14

ص   saad
صدف   sadaf

Shell

Strung out in a 45 NM/ 80 kilometre line, 25 NM offshore, lie the four main islands of the Halaniyyaat group, formerly called the Kuria Muria. They stand on the edge of the continental shelf, their waters, teeming with fish, fed by one of the world's major upwelling zones, where rich nutrients are forced up the continental slope by ocean currents from the 2,000-metre depths below. 50-tonne sperm whales spend hours feeding on giant squid in these depths before surfacing to replenish their oxygen supplies in a near-comatose state, where they become a hazard both to shipping and to themselves. The soft buff-coloured horizontally stratified cliffs of the largest island, Halaniyyah, tower above waters which are tranquil from November to April but become treacherous by June, when the south-west monsoon (*khareef*) raises considerable seas and makes navigation to them a hazardous undertaking. Avoiding the rough season, I went there by sea on a shell-hunting expedition in late 1995 to act as the liaison officer to one of the finest characters I met during my time in Oman.

Dr Donald Bosch, a decorated US World War Two veteran and missionary who served at the Battle of the Bulge, ran the Khoula Hospital Oman until he retired in 1983. He was one of the very few Westerners to be awarded the Order of Oman for his service to that nation and was granted Omani citizenship. At the award ceremony, he was gifted a house with servants in a cove in the hamlet of Haramel close to the old city of Musqat. It was here that he hosted regular and rigorous square-dancing sessions to which I and my wife, who was then superintendent of the physiotherapy department at his old hospital, do-si-doed as Don called out the changes in his soft southern-State drawl. He was an avid hunter and collector of Arabian seashells, one beautiful and hitherto unidentified example of which, *punctada eloise*, was named after his equally impressive wife, Eloise. I once asked him why the bases of seashells were often so beautifully marked even though they were seldom visible. He simply replied, 'Because The Almighty made them that way.' His unalloyed goodness was much admired by the Omani royal family. This was demonstrated when he and three other European conchologists were given the use of a Royal Navy of Oman landing ship, *Al Doghas*, to explore the shallow inshore waters of the Halaniyyah Islands in search of hitherto undiscovered shells.

In 1835, Hallaniyah was the only island in the group to be inhabited. Its seven families comprised twenty-three souls. Captain Haines reported that the men 'were of small stature, the women stout, and all very far from handsome'! Eighty years later, another maritime visitor used the shelter of the islands for a more nefarious purpose. The imperial German navy raider *SMS Königsberg* had captured the *SS City of Winchester* in August 1914 (the first allied marine casualty of the war). Having relieved the *Winchester* of its coal, whilst leaving its cargo of tea in place, the *Königsberg*'s crew detonated explosives in its engine room to send the sorry vessel to the seabed thirty metres below, assisted by firing three rounds into its hull. Today the wreck lies upright on the sea floor and is said to be home to a huge grouper, which welcomes intrepid divers who visit occasionally. These remarkable islands are home to not just sperm whales and groupers but a unique humpback whale population which unlike others of its kind does not migrate between low-latitude breeding and high-latitude feeding grounds. Although some of their number have been tracked on longer-range journeys to Yemeni and Indian waters, they tend to return to join their 100-strong group of cousins to feed and breed between the Halaniyyaat Islands and Masirah 230 NM to the north-east.

Countless seabirds nest in the towering cliffs of Hallaniyah. The flatter rock-strewn lowlands of the third largest island of Qibliyyah have been home for centuries to the blue-faced (and blue-footed) booby. These exotic birds have little to do but breed, eat, and defecate. These undisturbed deposits of guano were harvested as fertiliser in the late nineteenth century by 'volunteer' workmen from Africa and Yemen who lived in small stone shelters and operated large mechanical iron rakes towed across the surface by steam-powered winches. The guano was forked onto narrow-gauge railway trucks pulled by a miniature steam train to the loading dock on the sheltered north side of the island. I know this because when I visited during this expedition, the shell of the train stood forlornly by the dock while the rails had rusted to lines of undisturbed reddish powder along the perfectly preserved timber sleepers of the old railway track. Little did I know then that I would return fifteen years later to select the most appropriate site for a proposed lighthouse to guide shipping on its way to the newly planned port of Duqm south-west of Masirah. That story is in Chapter 24.

Sat a distance of 550 NM (1,000 km) north-west of Al-Hallaniyah, across the endless dunes of *rub al khali*, lie the once rich pearl banks which stretched in a broad ribbon from Abu Dhabi to Al-Jubail in Saudi Arabia. In these ten-to-thirty-metre sunlit shallows, harvesting saltwater pearls (*loolooah*) had been an 8000-year-old Gulf occupation since neolithic times. With the arid desert unable to support any meaningful level of commercial agriculture, pearl fishing was a major source of income. The principal pearling season was June to September. The crew of a typical vessel, a *sambuq* or *shu'i*, captained by a *nakhoda*, comprised nine men of whom four were pearl divers (*ghawasin*) and four their rope-handling assistants (*siyab*). The divers wore leather sheaths to protect their fingers and a nose-clip of bone, horn, or wood. When ready, they hooked a foot into a loop in a weighted rope and descended to the seabed up to thirty metres below for between thirty seconds and two minutes. When the catch was complete, the vessels sailed to a sandbank or local harbour, where the oysters were exposed to the sun to rot before the few pearls contained within them were gathered up and graded into three classes of six sizes, the finest of which, '*al-maha*', was named after 'the beautiful-eyed' oryx.

Pearls were relatively unknown in Europe until Cambyses II, son of Cyrus the Great, extended the Achaemenid Empire to Egypt in 525 BCE. Across the later Roman Empire, pearled jewels were highly desirable as symbols of wealth and status. They were exported along the maritime trade routes to be sold at Aleppo and Istanbul and from the seventh century CE onwards from Indian ports, principally Bombay (Mumbai), where buyers from as far as China would haggle over the finest examples. The fact that only one in about two thousand oyster shells contained a pearl of any real value shows how labour-intensive their recovery from the seabed must have been, particularly as a single diver could harvest a maximum of about twelve shells per dive. Put another way, just three to four pearls might be found in a tonne of shells harvested by individual free-swimming divers. Great moraines of shells found in an excavated sixth-century CE settlement in the Emirate of Umm Al Quwain confirmed how rare natural pearls are and why they had such value.

In later years, pearls were sold to local dealers, who traded them on at a considerable mark-up. Annual imports from India, via the principal regional emporium of Musqat, were paid for principally in pearls. S. B. Miles estimated that the annual revenue in the early twentieth century (derived from customs returns, etcetera) was between £500,000 and £750,000 (£79M to £118M today). He stated that the *nakhoda* kept twenty percent of the proceeds, the divers thirty and their assistants twenty percent between them, leaving ten percent for stores and equipment. The management and profits of the trade were, according to Miles, 'entirely in the hands of Hindoo and Khoja merchants' based in Bahrain, Musqat, and the coastal towns from Abu Dhabi to Ra's al Khaimah, who sold 'provisions, clothes and other necessities to the pearl fishers at exorbitant prices'. That ten percent share went straight back into the pockets of the wily dealers.

In the mid-sixteenth century, all native vessels were required to purchase a trading and pearling pass (*jawaaz*) from the Portuguese customs house and pay duty on goods landed. Incidentally, a 'passport' in Arabic is *jawaaz safar* ('journey pass'), an 'embassy' is *sifaara* and an 'ambassador', *safeer*. The excessive Portuguese response to those who did not meet their demands was uncompromising and generated hatred. Jihad was invoked and rebellion broke out in late 1521 and early 1522. The Portuguese factor in Bahrain was dragged from his office and crucified.

At the time of the factor's unfortunate demise, early maps of the Gulf were based principally on those of the second-century CE geographer Claudius Ptolemaeus. These named the island of Bahrain 'Ichara', possibly a variant of 'Icarus', although the early Arabs called it *awal*. A quarter of a century later, on a rare Venetian map in the collection of the Emir of Sharjah, which he showed me when I called on him in 2000, it is called 'baharam'. By the time that Arabs of *al-huwalah* tribe dominated Bahrain in the mid-eighteenth century, it was named 'Barahem' and by the end of that century 'Baharein', by which time import duties there had been removed, and its capital had become the centre of the Gulf pearl trade. As mentioned in Chapter Two, its Arabic name, *al-baḥrayn*, literally means 'The Two Seas'. Some say this comes from the two stretches of water which lie between the Qatar peninsula to the east and the Saudi mainland to the west. I prefer the less prosaic derivation of a saltwater sea above the pearl banks and a fresh-water sea below them. This is where fossil water which fell on the mountains of Yemen two thousand years ago had percolated through the tilted limestone Arabian Plate to collect in aquifers below the island before bubbling up through the seabed as densely cold fresh water springs.

Maps published by the London Society for the Diffusion of Useful Knowledge in 1831 note a 'pearl fishery' between 'Aradus' and 'Tylos' islands (Bahrain). The placename 'Catara' was shown on the mainland, but the Qatar peninsula had not yet appeared as a significant geographical feature on maps or charts. It was only from the mid-nineteenth century onwards that British charts depicted it properly, one from 1860 naming the peninsula 'BARB–AL–KATR'. Forty years after the publication of this remarkable document, which also charted the coast of Abu Dhabi in some detail for the first time, it has been estimated that sixty percent of that region's adult male population were employed in the pearling industry. Even in the early twentieth century, about a quarter of Gulf Arabs remained involved in it. The trade reached its zenith in 1912, the so-called 'Years of Superabundance', before trailing away in the middle of the last century as the exploitation of petrochemical products and the introduction of cultured pearls superseded pearling as the Gulf's principal natural resource.

***

The fossilised early predecessors of pearl-bearing molluscs lie locked in limestone on the 2,500-metre plateau of *al-jebel al-akhdar* (the Green Mountain), four hundred kilometres east of the pearl banks. The mountain range is named not so much for the coppery-green tinge of its rocks but for the numerous tiny green fields cultivated by the remarkable hill tribes who have lived in the region since antiquity. I camped there often in the early 1990s, once in an extremely rare snowstorm. This brought wonder and amazement to the children of the extended Arab family that eked out a living by weaving goat-hair rugs for sale in the souq in Nazwa before tourism became established. In the winter months, I donated blankets and warm clothing to the ever-vigilant matriarch as temperatures dipped towards zero and was rewarded with indescribably foul *qahwa* served in cups which had not seen a washing-up bowl in decades.

Two thousand metres below them to the south-east, on the *jiddat al harasis* escapement, once a coastal cliff, lie drifts of half-buried rudists – one-and-a-half-million-year-old reef-building bivalves from the Jurassic period. This remote area is home to a single massive dune over one hundred metres high, which creeps north-westwards, its fine sand grains blown up the wind-facing slope to fly up and fall down the huge crescent-shaped steeper slope which faces its eventual destination. I first climbed it in 1992, and by the time of my last visit in 2009, it had travelled twelve kilometres further inland, releasing acacia and prosopis trees from its grip. The latter gained all their moisture through their leaves, collecting morning dew and moisture from a weak onshore sea breeze to feed their deep roots. Both species provided browsing for the camels and goats of the local *bedu*, who claim this remarkable landscape as their *dar*. I had come to find the rudist fields hidden within the dunes and rock outcrops, which looked identical whichever way one faced.

Wishing to advertise my presence and cause no offence, I followed the most recent vehicle tracks to within half a kilometre of the *bedu* encampment and continued on foot, hand raised in greeting, to be welcomed cautiously by a young tribesman who assumed I was lost. As the womenfolk tittered hidden within the tent, he and his father fell about laughing when I explained I was looking for fossils (*al-a'hfouri*). They knew where they were, but why a crazy Englishmen with Jordanian-accented Arabic would want such things they knew not. My visit would doubtless be recounted again and again across the embers of their campfires – a stupid white-eye searching for stones in a stone-filled desert! Too much sun, my friend. They were of course right, but finding the fossils was worth the mockery. There were hundreds of thousands of them, the upper ones growing on the skeletons of those below. Most were about ten centimetres across at the mouth, tapering to a root a third of a metre below. Others had much larger diameters, forty centimetres across, and grew in marble-like spirals around a central vacant opening, once home to its hungry marine host as waves swept ashore above it. Some of these extraordinary stone bivalves now gaze skywards from my Japanese garden in West Sussex, perhaps to perplex archaeologists in some distant future.

CHAPTER 15

ض   daad
ضابط   daabit

Officer

I joined the Royal Navy in 1967 and specialised as a hydrographic surveyor four years later. My interest in hydrography was nurtured during my time as a midshipman in the ice patrol ship *HMS Endurance*, commanded by a captain who epitomised all which is good as a consummate seaman and leader of men. During a survey in uncharted Antarctic waters, he sent me by Whirlwind Mk.9 helicopter to raise a huge marker flag on a rocky islet jutting above the surrounding pack ice. On my return he studied the flag streaming in the wind through his binoculars and turning to me with kindly eyes said, 'You should be a proud young man, Bennett, for you are the first person ever to set foot on that piece of land.' I stammered a thank you, saluted and returned to my duties with an increased sense of excitement in the life I had chosen. This was reinforced further during that deployment when I assisted in the initial survey of the *SS Great Britain*, lying as a hulk in Sparrow Cove in the Falkland Islands, its cavernous interior just a network of iron struts and crossmembers. I was nineteen years old.

Twenty-one years later, in the autumn of 1990, I was studying colloquial Arabic at the Army School of Languages, Beaconsfield, prior to being posted on loan service to Oman. Saddam Hussein's invasion of Kuwait had added impetus to the acquisition of new vocabulary. I had learned my earliest Arabic from my Palestinian nanny when I lived in Jordan as a child. I thought this basic knowledge would have set me in good stead when six years earlier as staff navigator to the Mine-Countermeasures Squadron based in Rosyth, I had been sent to assist a major mine clearance task during OPERATION HARLING in the Gulf of Suez.

Armed with what I thought was an impressive array of phrases and knowing that no conversation is started in Arabia without first shaking hands, I opened my conversation with the local Egyptian naval commodore. Having wished him a peaceful life and thanked God that everything was fine, I continued my introduction. Suddenly his eyebrows rose in some alarm. Then the corners of his eyes creased up and breaking into a smile and perfect English he said, 'Do you know what you have just said, O Estefen?'

'I think so, *sidee* ("sir"),' I replied, 'but please excuse my bad Arabic. If I have said the wrong thing, I learnt it from my mother's maid when I was young.'

'Your mother's maid spoke not gutturally, dear Estefan, but from the gutter! She has taught you many rude words. Let us proceed in your mother's tongue; it will be safer.'

So, suitably abashed, I later determined not only to grasp the essentials of colloquial Arabic but to understand more of the people who spoke it and the land in which they lived. I had, for instance, no idea at that stage that in common with my own maritime travels, Arabia had been to Antarctica and back as I mentioned in Chapter Two. I was also to learn that more than just a smattering of Arabic could be a considerable advantage to a royal naval officer on loan service. In 1982, the same year as I saw service in the Falklands War, Britain signed a memorandum of understanding with Oman which set out rules for the provision of loan service personnel. Many of the senior Omani military had reservations about some of the 'advisors' who had been sent, preferring in many cases the contract mercenaries whose allegiance they could rely on. General Glubb had also been critical of the way British military missions (loan service forebears) were staffed, reporting that 'a three-year secondment is not enough to allow an officer to learn Arabic, much less to be familiar with the Arab outlook and mentality and to mingle with them socially'. He considered that officers with long experience of Arabs were 'infinitely preferable', and 'an unwise choice of tactless British officers has at times produced against [Britain] an undeserved but not incomprehensible hatred'.

It has been said that those who work with Arabs either get to like them or get like them. I fall into both categories and have twice been condemned as 'having gone native', somewhat unfairly in my opinion. Having not been born into the harsh desert climate, where a fatalistic approach to life is essential for survival, I do not possess the inner steel necessary to go fully native in Arabia. That said, I found some of the chilly indifference of twenty-first-century England less appealing than the warm hospitality and courtesy I had left behind. This chapter touches on some of the remarkable officers and leaders, both Arabic and British, who left their positive footprint in the sands of Arabia or who adumbrated its life and history to an otherwise less-informed Western world, the Arab attitude to which forms much of the content of Chapter 19. I have already quoted from several of these remarkable men, chiefly T. E. Lawrence, Lieutenant-General Sir John Bagot Glubb, and Wilfred Thesiger and would recommend strongly their works and others listed in the bibliography at the back of this book.

One such officer was William Baffin, born of humble origins in 1584 and who served as chief pilot of an expedition in 1612 seeking the north-west passage. Three years later he navigated the *Discovery* through the Davis Strait and into the vast bay which bears his name. It has been reported that he may have been the first navigator to obtain an accurate longitude at sea from lunar observations. He subsequently conducted surveys for the East India Company as their fleet navigator and tragically was one of just two Englishmen killed during the shore bombardment of the Portuguese fort on the island of Qeshm while taking ranges ashore with his survey instruments. The Portuguese commander was Admiral Dom Ruy Freire de Andrade, whom Lorimer described as a man 'more politic than conscientious and rather more feared than beloved'. I met one or two such senior officers during my royal naval service, but for the life of me, I cannot recall their names.

Another much-admired predecessor of mine, whose comments feature throughout this book, combined consummate diplomacy with brilliant hydrographic ability. This was Captain Stafford Bettesworth Haines, Indian Navy, who was commanded by the Bombay government in 1834 to try and purchase the island of Socotra from the local shaykh as a coaling station because 'a direct communication by steam' [from India to Suez] was 'the anxious object of the Supreme Government of India'.

In this he was initially unsuccessful, but no international feathers were ruffled, the shaykh saying on Haines' departure, 'God is witness we have both endeavoured to fulfil our respective duties: you to your government and I to my tribe, as their father. Farewell.'

For 500 years, the interior of Oman had been ruled by the self-styled *malik* ('king') of the *nabhani* dynasty, although one Arab historian noted rather harshly that 'of the rulers of the *bani-nabhi*, there was not one *malik* whom the God of grace and benevolence could approve of'. By contrast, Ibn Battuta found the *nabhani* ruler he met at Nizwa in the mid-sixteenth century to be 'a man of superior qualities'. Another such man was Ahmad bin Sa'id bin Muhammad, whose tribe, the *al bu-sa'id*, was part of the *hinawi* confederation. He was born in Adam, a village on the northern fringes of *al-jiddat al-harasis* at the turn of the eighteenth century. Having distinguished himself in the service of earlier Imams, he was appointed *wali* of Sohar in 1737. His majlis was in the rectangular white-washed multi-storeyed donjon of Sohar's central fort, which withstood the best which mid-eighteenth-century siege warfare could throw at it. Ahmed bin Sa'id's strategic vision ended Persian occupation of Oman in perpetuity. His descendants have been ruling Oman to this day.

Two early twentieth-century chroniclers of Arabia brought its history and ethnography to a wider Western audience. The less well-known Colonel Samuel Barrett Miles, Indian Army and Political Service, was appointed as political agent and consul in Musqat (subsequently Political Agent Turkish Arabia) in October 1872. He remained there for fourteen years, the same amount of time that I spent in the region as an adult. This was a turbulent time for Miles, particularly as tribes in the interior continued to foment trouble after the Sultan had succumbed to British pressure to end the trade in East African slaves a year after his arrival. The situation was exacerbated by the spread of Ottoman authority over the Gulf littoral region as far as the Qatar peninsula in the year before he took up his post. Following the examples of earlier explorers of Oman's interior, from Ibn Battuta in the sixteenth century to Lieutenants Wellstead and Whitelock three centuries later, Miles journeyed extensively throughout Oman and wrote an account of his travels and research in his retirement. Although its title is *The Countries and Tribes of the Persian Gulf*, it deals mainly with Oman, a country (so the introduction to the 1965 second edition tells us) he knew 'better than any other European had known before him, or until very recent times, has known since'. It is hoped that the latter comment acknowledged Thesiger's significant contribution, let alone that of Jan Morris, whose account of the 1955 meeting with the 'Sultan in Oman' is told superbly.

A much more significant reference work is the two-volume British Government of India's *Gazetteer of the Persian Gulf: Oman and Central Arabia*, the first volume of which covered the history of that area from 1507, the year that Affonso de Albuquerque rounded Ra's al Hadd. The man responsible was the polyglot Scot, John Gordon Lorimer, of the Indian Civil Service. He was commissioned to compile a classified guide for diplomats so that their judgements and reports could be based on the best background possible. It was not declassified until 1955 but thereafter acknowledged as a masterwork. Volume Two, covering the geography of the region, was published in 1908, six years before he died under tragic circumstances while serving as the British political resident in Bushire just before the outbreak of the First World War. Volume One of this exquisitely researched guide was published the year after his death. Lorimer was held in the highest regard by all who knew him, of whatever race. Although his obituary could not acknowledge his magnificent contribution to our understanding of Arabia because it was still classified 'secret' at the time of his death, his legacy remains, and I among many others am thankful for it.

Before my appointment to Oman, I had been the officer-in-charge of the international naval Hydrographic School based in *HMS Drake*, Devonport. The last British loan service admiral commanding the Royal Navy of Oman (RNO) informed the Ministry of Defence in Whitehall that the Omanis, with their long mainly unsurveyed coastline, wished to establish a hydrographic capability of their own. I was therefore sent out to Musqat with the remit to write the specifications for such a task, based broadly on the equipment fitted in my last ship, *HMS Roebuck*. This I did, and I met the deputy commander of their navy, His Highness Shihab bin Tariq Al Said, for the first time. One could not but warm to him. No swear words on this occasion, I am pleased to report. Much against my pre-visit briefing in Whitehall, I advised His Highness that there was little point in acquiring a modern surveying vessel if his navy had no specialists to man and operate it. I proposed a longer-term project, starting with the recruitment and training of selected Omani officers and ratings to gain the necessary competencies before a major capital expenditure programme was instigated. My report was submitted, and I returned to Devon as Saddam Hussein was rattling sabres in the north of the Gulf. The British admiral retired. His deputy, the Sultan's cousin, became Commander RNO, and I, being unencumbered by marriage, was posted first to Beaconsfield then to Oman as the first Omani Hydrographer. My initial appointment was for two years. Glubb was right. I stayed for six.

Many of the Arabic officers I encountered professionally were remarkable men. Two of them went through six tough months of academic study on the long hydrographic course at *HMS Drake*, including during the Holy Month of Ramadhan, without complaint, loss of concentration, or spiritual integrity. That first glass of water at sunset each day during Ramadhan must have been extraordinarily welcome. With that sort of physical and mental courage, it goes without saying that they both passed the course with honours. But the Arab officer to whom I owe the most is one whose name I never learnt. He was an Egyptian army helicopter pilot, who flew me from our base at Adabiyah during OPERATION HARLING to Zafaarana on the Red Sea coast. My recce had gone well. We climbed back into the helicopter for the return flight. Then at 500 feet and 80 knots, a mist started to form on the curved glass dome in front of the pilot to creep upwards before drips condensed and fell on his gloves, arms, and legs. He muttered something under his breath, which doubtless my nanny would have understood, before pushing the cyclic forward to descend at some speed towards the desert floor rising rapidly to greet us. Landing in a cloud of swirling sand, he jumped out, pulled at some wiring and, with not inconsiderable effort, jettisoned the culprit, a leaking lead-acid battery. Sand was heaped beneath his feet to absorb what it could and we took off again as if nothing significant had happened. Back at the base in Adabiyah, I tried to shake his hand, but his blisters forbade it. So we just smiled at each other, and with many 'shukraans' on my part went our separate ways. I probably owe him my life, so *shukran* again, my dear brother-in-arms.

CHAPTER 16

ط   taa'
طريق   tareeq

Trail

The mountains and deserts of Arabia are criss-crossed with narrow ways and trails formed by pedestrians, pack animals (both camels and donkeys), gazelles, and more recently, mechanical graders, which connect remote villages and oases to centres of civilisation. One such centre was *'ubar*, the so-called 'Atlantis of the Sands', supposedly rediscovered during a space shuttle flight, as the focus from which faint camel caravan trails radiated outwards. My scepticism remains intact. However I have followed hundreds of these trails in Oman and the UAE both on foot and in a 4WD and have been captured by the lingering presence of the souls that preceded me along these ancient mountain and lowland tracks, just as I feel now when walking along the South Downs Way, which runs across chalk hills behind my home in the UK.

Caravan trails have wound their way from the ancient ports on the south-eastern coast of the Arabian Sea, through the Hadhramaut to Marib, Mecca, Medina, and beyond. They ran from the Gulf littoral past the borders of the *rub al-khali, al-dahna* and *an-nafud* sands to Riyadh, Ha'il and Al Jawf. These ancient cities are now connected by a network of black-topped roads, but most of them are much younger than my children, who used to bounce along beside me as we negotiated the old twisted coastal track from Quriyat to Sur, fifty miles to the south-east. Chinese contractors created a modern coastal highway to replace it, but the old trail twenty-five years ago remained ungraded, demanding and spectacular. To landward tower the 'lofty ranges' of the eastern *hajar ash-sharqi*, as the Portuguese conqueror,

Affonso d' Albuquerque, described them. On the other, a series of snow-white sandy coves are interspersed with tiny fishing villages straddling the dry riverbeds which debouch from the great gorges which carry their names: *wadi dayqah*, *wadi 'arba'een* ('forty'), the spectacularly beautiful *wadi shab*, and *wadi halwi*. But *wadi* are not always dry. Once every few years, gigantic storm clouds gather over the mountains and discharge thousands of tons of hard rain to cascade down the sides of the valleys in boiling brown flash floods. The force of these infrequent but overpowering events has carved sheer-sided chasms out of the grey-brown limestone mountains.

One of the more remarkable is *wadi qalhat*, once home to thousands of horses transported by sea from the Dhofar region for onward shipment to India. From its mouth extends a narrow fan-shaped lagoon, once a teeming harbour, its brackish green-brown water now retained by an undredged sandbar at its seaward end. By the time of Marco Polo's visit in 1292, Qalhat was under Persian Hormuzi control. He noted that it was a 'great city with a haven that is large and good and is frequented by numerous ships with goods from India'. Forty years later, Ibn Battuta also travelled to the walled city of 'Kilhat' by foot from Sur. Having gained admission from the gatekeeper standing before the 'lance high' wall which snakes up the mountainside, he was taken to 'the Ameer of the city, a man of politeness and good qualities'. He reported that Qalhat stood 'on an eminence overlooking the sea and the harbour; it was built by Bibi [Lady] Miriam. The meaning of Bibi among them is freeborn'. The buff-coloured cube-shaped mausoleum of Bibi Maryam with its collapsed tiered roof exposing the once beautifully defined interior still retained an element of grandeur when I last visited it in 2009. So too did the remarkable arched stone roof of the water cistern which stands close by. Water vapour still condensed on the roof's cool interior and dripped into the pool below, generating deep-toned echoes. Both structures overlook the old harbour and the ruins of the ancient walled city, which are now just mounds of rubble. Despite the modern highway which runs behind the ruins, it takes little imagination to evoke the sights, sounds, and smells of this once prosperous city as one wanders through the just discernible streets littered with sixteenth-century pottery shards.

The Author with his Mother outside the Tomb of Bibi Maryam – 1994

Ibn Battuta later travelled up the southern of the two great arterial highways that ran from the coast into the interior or *al-joof* on either side of the Jebal Akhdar Massif. His trail followed the 200-kilometre-long *wadi* complex, which cuts through the eastern Hajar mountain range and became the traditional route between Musqat and *al-joof*. Orders for the construction of the great rubble-filled round tower at Nazwa, which Ibn Battuta had visited three centuries before, were sent out from Iman Sultan bin Saif al-Ya'ribi's castle at Rustaq, which guarded the northern trading route. According to the records of Milburn and Thornton's 1825 *Oriental Commerce*, goods from the interior were carried down these tracks comprising 'almonds, cattle, drugs of all sorts, various gums, hides, honey, skins, wax, pearl-shells, horses and raisins'. The return caravans to Nazwa bore 'Indian commodities principally ginger, grain, opium, piece-goods, pepper, sugar, spices, turmeric, and European cutlery, glassware, looking-glasses and broadcloth'. Given the value of such cargoes, mounted guards, *askari*, were doubtless in close attendance.

These trading and raiding routes needed protection. It was the Portuguese who had ordered the construction of forts (*hisn*) from Ra's al Hadd to the head of the Gulf based on designs which used Italian advances in ballistic technology. The three forts at Musqat were built to plans produced by the Milanese architect, C. B. Cairate. Two of them, Fort Capitan and St Joao (now *hisn mirani and jalani*), guarded the cove, and the other the adjacent anchorage at Muttrah. Earlier Arab forts, such as the one at Sohar, were characterised by a rectangular wall with a round tower at each corner. The design relied on a large garrison to man the walls and towers. The improved Italian design was based around one central tower in which a limited number of defenders could operate superior artillery pieces imported from Europe. Alterations to these forts post-1650 gave them their present appearance.

Sultan bin Saif (who died in 1718) built a beautiful and extraordinary thirty-metre-square fort at Hazm between Rustaq and the sea, which now shelters his remains. I trekked to the fort just after the first Gulf War and paid my respects to this extraordinary leader as I scanned the Batinah plain from the northerly of the two circular cannon-carrying towers built on opposing corners of the structure. The Portuguese forts at Musqat, and the factory where the bulk of the ammunition and stores was held, were seized in the mid-seventeenth century. Two vessels were captured in the khawr; the others weighed anchor and sailed away. Their forts and watchtowers remain, but hardly a trace of Portuguese culture is discernible in Arabia. The Portuguese flag, once that of a regional power, became, as Lorimer so perfectly put it, 'the ensign of a distant and foreign nation'.

There is a faint trail which climbs from the old fortified outer wall of Musqat over the mountains and down again to the back of the modern industrial estate at *al-wadi al-kabir* (the Big Wadi) once the location of Musqat's first airport. It has nothing to commend it in the way of beauty or particular interest apart from it being the earliest route towards the network of trails which led to the interior. It is one of hundreds which I followed during my time in Oman, each one leaving a distinct memory. On that occasion it was an unexpected encounter with the resident pack of wild dogs which had made it their home, though they were kept at bay with a few well-aimed stones. Another more spectacular but equally hazardous trail was to the rough stone houses and tiny terraces built into the cliff one thousand metres above the floor of *wadi ghul* (literally 'ghoul'), often referred to as Oman's 'Grand Canyon'. The path descends gently from the village at the eastern end of *al-jebel al-akhdar* (where I had delivered warm clothing to its matriarch) to traverse a scree-filled slope, which narrows to a few metres across. This affords, should one wish it, an uninterrupted view of the village of Nakr hundreds of metres below. The villagers who farmed these terraces until quite recently accessed them using ladders of solid acacia branches jammed into narrow vertical fissures leading to the plateau of Jebal Shams a hundred metres above. I grasped the lower rungs, but the dizzying climb was way outside my comfort zone. Perhaps less well-known are the trails from the summit of the adjacent *saiq* plateau leading to tiny mud-and-stone houses huddled against the cliffs of Wadi Qashah, fed ingeniously by a *falaj* system carrying water to them from a distant spring.

Away from the mountains and across the plains, main routes are built on embanked black-top roads designed to permit the wind to blow away any significant accumulation of sand. Radiating off the highways, graded trails often peter out, overrun by trains of dunes heading inexorably downwind. Satellite navigation is of little use here, as previously recorded wilderness trails have simply disappeared. But the Arab guides who led Harry St John Philby, Bertram Thomas and Wilfred Thesiger through the *rub al-khali*, and the *bedu* tribes to which they belonged, seemed to have these trails hard-wired into their brains. The ever-watchful Polaris to the north and the rising sun in the east would of course have provided cardinal reference points, but so did the shape of certain distinctive dunes and trees, the latter half-submerged in a seemingly identical sandscape.

Within these areas, particularly as one closes the coast, can be found that most treacherous of terrain, *sabkha*. The outline of a graded road may stretch across its flattened surface, but beneath that seemingly hard-crusted top layer lies a salty sea of liquid mud ready to snare the wheels of any unwary traveller's 4WD. I encountered a number of stretches of *sabkha* along the Gulf littoral and when traversing the *jiddat al-harasis* or limits of the Wahiba sands en-route to an intended coastal location. The technique is to approach the edge of the depression and park. Walk out across the crusty surface to test any subsidence or sign of the reddish-brown mud. Then if all seems well, drive slowly across the *sabkha* with the windows open, listening carefully for any sign of cracking. Of course driving through sand itself is not straightforward without having lowered the tyre pressure and avoiding sudden acceleration or breaking. Even the most inconspicuous-looking dune may conceal a three-metre dip on its far side, so unless you enjoy airborne driving and a shattered suspension, advance with caution!

Memorable *sabkha* fields lie astride the trails across the *barr al-hickman*, the rhombic-shaped flat peninsula on the mainland to the west of Masirah. The beaches here are stunning with flamingo-filled lagoons lining its southern coast. Humpback whales dive in the deeper offshore waters and dugongs graze the *hashish* (grass) forests inshore. I have often camped there in this birdwatchers' paradise, having first negotiated the rutted trails across sun-hardened concrete-like *sabkha* but never during the windy *khareef* season. This is when the trails liquify and unwary travellers rue the day they drove into their unremitting grip. However all would not be lost, because the local garage owner in the village of Mahoot, thirty kilometres to the north, would get to hear of the problem and be delighted to extricate the sorry vehicle and its owner for a non-negotiable and completely unreasonable consideration.

About two years after I arrived in Oman on loan service, the government signed a contract with the Indian Naval Hydrographic Service to survey the coast between Quriyat and Sur, for which I developed the specifications. Part of my research required me to fly along that coast in a Royal Air Force of Oman helicopter to determine the general lay of the terrain and possible extent of its off-lying reefs. Great ribbons and trails of tomato-soup-coloured algal bloom or 'red tide' greeted our aerial arrival, created by an upwelling of nutrient-rich water from the ocean deeps off Ra's al Hadd. The water was otherwise crystal-clear, revealing dense shoals of fish chased by black-tipped reef sharks. Photographs and measurements were taken and recorded. Back in my offices in *muaskar al-murtafa'a* I spread out the medium-scale army land maps and annotated them with my observations. And there, halfway between two small coastal villages, was a perfect beach, clearly covered at high tide and seemingly inaccessible by land.

Undeterred, I set off to find it taking Annie, 'wife of Bennett', with me. We left the graded track running about a kilometre inland and headed seawards across the flat, stony plain, causing a family of Arabian gazelles to scatter in alarm. We soon reached the four-metre-high cliffs standing above where I considered the beach to be. It appeared initially that our way was barred by a sharp rocky outcrop covered in thorny scrub, so we left the vehicle and walked up over it. There below us lay the most beautiful arc of shell-strewn sand with countless rock pools beyond it. A flat brownish-grey rock about the size of a snooker table jutted out over the undercut cliff, a perfect potential camping site with no one in view but a pair of ospreys nesting on the nearest small headland to the north.

It took a while and some rock shifting to find the only suitable trail for the vehicle, but find it we did. This became 'Annie's beach', furnished, in time, with a kitchen range fashioned from flat stones and a driftwood storage area. My comprehensive camping crate fashioned from a wooden ammunition case completed the ensemble. We returned there shortly after our return to Oman nine years later. Apart from the fireplace being overgrown, it had changed not one bit, with no tyre tracks visible anywhere in its vicinity. When we drove down to spend another weekend there a month later, our supply of driftwood had been replenished. This could only have been done by local villagers as a token of Arabic hospitality. So we had never really been alone there and were welcomed back without a word being spoken. Typically and wonderfully Arabian.

CHAPTER 17

ط   dhaa'
ظهر   dh'uhr

Noon

At ten in the morning on mid-summer's day 1995, our white, red and green spinnaker, emblazoned with crossed swords and a curved dagger, or *khunjar*, snapped full from a brisk onshore breeze as the forty-foot-long yacht, *u'qab* ('eagle'), raced southwards past an islet festooned with strips of red bunting on our starboard beam. They had been placed there, as they had been since antiquity, by local fishermen in honour of an ancient sea spirit, because certain rocks, trees, and wells were said to have divine properties. Continuing to honour or appease ancient spirits in remote locations in the late twentieth century is an indication of how deep-seated some of those beliefs are. But for now the aim was to cross the 23° 27' degree of northerly latitude – the Tropic of Cancer – at exactly noon, when the solstice sun would be vertically overhead. We achieved the aim with precision and celebrated expansively afterwards with a pod of resident spinner dolphins spiralling clear of the sea around us for company.

Noon (*dh'uhr*) is one of the five fixed times when the mu'adhdhin, or *muezzin*, calls the faithful to prayer, or *salah*. The others are at dawn (*fajr*) just before sunrise, *asr* in the late afternoon, just after sunset (*maghrib*), and *ishr* before retiring at night. The call to prayer always commences with the twice-repeated exhortation to acknowledge that 'God is most great'. This is followed by, 'I testify that there is no God but God. I testify that Muhammad is God's apostle. Come to prayer, come to salvation; prayer is better than sleep'[included in the dawn call] and closed with the repeated exhortation that 'God is most Great. There is no God but God'.

The first *muezzin* was considered to be an early convert, the black slave, Bilal, whose Meccan owner had weighted him down with stones in the glare of the sun. Despite this, he refused to recant, testifying loudly that there is no God but Allah. Prayer was initially conducted facing east but then changed to the direction of Jerusalem after Muhammad's 'Night Journey' on the mythical winged donkey, *buraq*. Facing the revered stone building in Mecca, the *ka'bah* followed later, when Muhammad felt commanded to increase the number of daily prayers from three to five. The Shi'a still maintain three prayer times following verse (*sura*) 17:78 in the Quran.

The Holy Quran and the traditions of its Prophet give to a Muslim a complete code of spiritual, personal, social, and legal behaviours. Apart from the profession of faith (*ash-shahada*) and prayer five times a day, the five 'Pillars of Islam' insist that the faithful must fast (*sawm*), especially from sunrise to sunset, during the Holy Month of Ramadhan, give alms (*zakaat*) to the poor, originally one fortieth of a man's annual income, and go on pilgrimage (*hajj*) to Mecca. This makes that city the holiest of all Islamic locations and control of Mecca carries with it considerable kudos. Its guardian was known as *ish-shereef* – 'The Sherif'.

It has been reliably estimated that in the sixteenth century, thirty to forty thousand pilgrims from the Maghreb region in North Africa and Egypt journeyed annually from *qahira* (Cairo) and two thirds that number travelled from Damascus. Mecca-bound pilgrims arrived in the southern entrepôts of Arabia or sailed across the Red Sea to the *hajj* ports of Yanbu, Al-Rabigh, and Jeddah in modern Saudi Arabia. The last of these had been under the control of an Ottoman governor since 1517. Logistic support and funds for both pilgrims and inhabitants was sent by sea from Constantinople to Cairo under the charge of a high Ottoman official. On the appointed day a gun would signal the start of the great pilgrimage. The *amir al-hajj* carried with him on a ceremonial wooden frame called the *mahmal*, an embroidered damask cloth, the *kiswa*, which had been used to cover the *ka'bah* in the 'Age of Ignorance'. Tens of thousands of pilgrims would follow the prince of the Hajj across the Sinai and down the ancient Hejaz coastal trading route towards Mecca. To deter *bedu* raids, tribal shaykhs were given honorary status, and 'subsidies' were paid to other potential raiders. Caravanserai were garrisoned. The other great hajj caravan departed from Damascus. It passed through Tebuk and Meddyin Salih, where (so Doughty, who accompanied them, reported) 'the weary Damascenes, inhabitants of a river city, fell to diligently washing their sullied garments'. The pilgrim-carrying Ottoman Hejaz railway, which Lawrence later attacked so successfully, started construction in 1901. To the south, Asian pilgrims were shipped in overcrowded steamers to Aden in their thousands, as every reader of Conrad's 'Lord Jim' will confirm. The fact that Peter O'Toole played both Lawrence and Jim is merely a coincidence!

Some of the sacred rites followed during *hajj*, such as the circumambulation of the ka'bah, were adopted then adapted by Muhammed when he made the annual pilgrimage to Mecca from Medina in 632 CE. His observances, such as the sunset prayer at the clearing of Muzdalifa, stoning representations of *shaytan* (Satan), and the ritual sacrifice on the final day, are followed by millions of Muslims to this day. The ka'bah, Well of Zamzam and the small square stone associated with Ibrahim (*maqam ibrahim*) are all enclosed within the *haram ish-sharif* – the 'Noble Sanctuary' – the world's largest mosque, capable of holding over one million pilgrims. There are plans to expand that to two and a half million. Just imagine.

A place of assembly, or *jama'a*, such as the great square in Marrakesh – Jemma al Fnaa – gives its name to that for a mosque (*masjid*). The English word 'mosque' is derived from the old Portuguese *mesquita*, which itself is derived from *masjid*. Friday (*yawn al-juma'a*) is the day of gathering in a large mosque (also called a *jama'a*) to hear the weekly *khutbah*, or sermon, from a spiritual leader, or *imam* – literally one who sets an example. This message often contains government-approved notices, not all of which are necessarily endorsed by the congregation.

The ninety-nine-year rule of the Umayyad dynasty, so strongly condemned by Ayatollah Khomeini in his 1981 book, *Islam and Revolution*, did however bequeath a cultural legacy which includes three great centres of worship – two in Jerusalem and one in Damascus. In Jerusalem, the great domed and colonnaded 'Dome of the Rock' was constructed on the platform formed from the ruins of the old Hebrew temple using the skills of Byzantine Christian stonemasons and artisans. The second is the silver-domed *al-aqsa* ('distant' or 'farthest') mosque. After Jerusalem fell under Ottoman control in 1517, Süleyman the Magnificent had both their external walls decorated with coloured Iznik tiles. In Damascus the 'Great Mosque' was built over the site of the fourth-century CE Christian church of St John the Baptist, itself contained within an earlier Roman 300-by-400-metre precinct. This magnificent mosaic-adorned mosque, lit by six hundred shimmering lamps, contains the tomb of Salah al-Din Yusuf ibn Ayyub (Saladin), the great twelfth-century CE Muslim general and hero of the Third Crusade. Dante in his 'Divine Comedy' placed both Muhammad and his successor, Ali, in the Circle of the Sowers of Discord, whereas he placed Saleh al-Din with other unbaptised but virtuous men in the first circle, Limbo, where Dante saw 'great Saladin, aloof alone'.

On a less grand scale than the mighty *jama'a*, I visited a tiny white-washed four-hundred-year-old four-domed mosque on the outskirts of the Fujairah Emirate village of Bidiya. This is famed for its bustling Thursday (*yawm al-khamis* – 'the fifth day') market and crumbling two-towered fort. Despite its size, the mosque had all the features common to such buildings including external washing facilities in which *wudu'* ('ritual cleansing') can be conducted. Within its carpeted interior is a *mihrab* (an 'alcove', also an Arabic-derived word) indicating the direction (*qibla*) to face when praying towards the ka'bah. Larger mosques contain a pulpit or *minbar*, several of which Salah al-Din donated to the great mosques of his day. The interiors of mosques are often masterpieces of Islamic architecture. Representations of human or animal forms, which might distract the worshipper, are replaced by abstract designs in stained glass. Sparkling chandeliers and polished brass lanterns are suspended from the ceilings and round the walls run exquisite ribbons of ceramic tiles and friezes of perfect Quranic calligraphy in dazzling gold-leaf.

Men and women pray separately. When not led collectively, a newly arrived worshipper joins the line of those already in prayer and declares quietly how many times he or she will complete the cycle of genuflection and prostration. Newcomers then continue their cycle in phase with other worshippers. After the final cycle, and after any private prayers, he or she will whisper *as-salaam alaykum* (peace be upon you) to those on either side and then leave. This coordinated quiet arrival and departure gives cohesion and a sense of unending continuity to the prayer ritual. Non-Muslims, having cleansed themselves appropriately, are welcome to watch from the sidelines to absorb something of this spiritual experience.

Prayer may be performed in any untainted place. Some Islamic scholars consider it forbidden (*haram*) to pray near where camels have settled for the night, because these are said to be frequented by *shaytan*. No such constraint was exercised during a courtesy visit by a Royal Naval frigate to Ra's al Khaimah, six months before the 2001 Twin Tower bombings. One of the ruler's sons, the chief of police and a powerful man in his early forties, invited me and the ship's impressive commanding officer to fly in his brand-new private Polish helicopter to a deserted village high up on a plateau near the summit of the mountain range which dominates the city, where he kept his beehives. Muhammed, like Sampson before him, was said to have a particular liking for honey (*'asl*), and many Muslims, like our shaykh, follow his example in its enjoyment. His bees, imported from Australia, generated 120 kilograms of acacia-tree-blossom honey from ten hives every two weeks. On a flat grey limestone promontory, jutting out over the steep scree slopes of Wadi Bi'h, we witnessed our host and two members of his staff perform the simple *salat al-asr* ('afternoon prayer'), conducted when a shadow is the same length of the object which casts it. After the Exordium, the first *surah* of the Quran, they bowed, straightened up, and sank gently to their knees before prostrating twice, hands on the warm rock either side of their heads. We two Christian naval officers, fellow Peoples of the Book, stood quietly behind them, looking across the dramatic chasm of Wadi Bi'h, feeling very small as Tawny Eagles circled lazily overhead.

My experience was not always so magical. Just before lunch with the American ambassador in Sana'a fifteen years ago, my wife and I were deafened by the call to prayer from the neighbouring mosque which, much to the chagrin of its disgruntled *muezzin*, directly abutted the more recently constructed embassy wall. To register his displeasure he had swung the loudspeakers away from the faithful and directly towards the adjoining ambassador's residence. This tone-deaf individual delighted in haranguing his infidel neighbours through low-quality speakers at maximum volume for twenty minutes at noon every Friday. The translated content of his sermon condemned the Americans to everlasting damnation, though which of Dante's circles of hell they would reside in remained uncertain.

CHAPTER 18

ع   ayn
عبد   a'bd

Slave

It came as something of a surprise to me when I was addressed as 'Abdullah' by some Arabs on our first meeting before they learned my given name. However, it is perfectly acceptable, indeed courteous, for them to call you 'Abdullah' – 'Slave of God' – as we are all surely that! But ignorance of cultural differences can cause offence, albeit unintended. Only the unwisest and least courteous of Westerners should call any Arab 'Abdul', for it simply means 'his slave'.

Slavery has been a fact of life, albeit a very challenging one, since one group of humans met a rival group. Nigel Biggar, in his clearsighted ethical study of colonialism, noted that from today's perspective, slavery is wrong, but 'to most of our ancestors up to the second half of the eighteen century, slavery was a fact of life – an institution that had existed all over the world since time immemorial'. It was prevalent in an unrestricted form in Arabia until it was recognised that the natural condition of followers of Islam was liberty. Only infidels captured in a holy war could be enslaved. Albert Hourani, in his *History of the Arab Peoples*, noted that slavery was a status recognised by Islamic law, and 'although slaves did not possess the legal rights of free men, shari'a [law] laid down that they should be treated with justice and kindness'. In an ordered Arabian society based on Quranic teaching, slaves had clear rights. They could marry among themselves if they chose to do so, and should a Moslem wish to marry a converted female slave, she first had to be freed.

Slaves were to be treated generously and humanely, provided with medical attention, and supported in old age. Once part of the household, domestic staff were integrated into the family unit and often chose to remain within it, even when freed, as they were guaranteed secure housing and sustenance. The Quran revealed in *surah* 33:50 that female slaves were a divine gift. Young female slaves were the most sought after for their value as concubines, and many of them became the mothers of famous rulers. The historian, Bernard Lewis, tells us that during the Second (Umayyad) Caliphate from 661 to 750 CE, when spoils from the Conquests had fed the coffers in Medina and Mecca, it had created a sybaritic society where 'slave girls and dancers vied with free Arab ladies for the attentions of the dissolute heirs of the warriors of the faith'.

The history of the Atlantic slave trade has been extensively reported, not least by objective historians like Hugh Thomas. The history of the East African slave trade has received less coverage in the West, although Lewis touches on it in his comprehensive account, *The Middle East*. His argument that the humanising effect of Islamic legislation after the Arabian Conquests led inadvertently to the 'large scale, long-range commerce in human beings' is hard to ignore. Anti-slavery action by European powers in Arabia in the early nineteenth century, as Thomas wisely said, was a lesser priority than the Atlantic trade, 'at least until West Africa had been bullied, bribed, or persuaded into morality'.

Because the Arabian Peninsula, unlike Caribbean Islands, the Southern United States or Brazil does not have the agricultural land which a slave workforce could be exploited to cultivate, the majority of slaves in Arabia entered enforced domestic, industrial, or military service. Others formed part of the crews of pearling vessels. Some slaves, however, had been sent out to work the land such as those who forcibly drained the marshes of Southern Iraq during the Baghdad-based Abbasid Caliphate in the ninth century CE, where mistreatment could have unwanted consequences. A very well recorded rebellion in southern Iraq by disaffected citizens and Bantu-speaking black slaves, the *zanji* (who were certainly not treated with 'justice and kindness'), flared up in 869 and was not quashed until 883. Thousands died though others later joined the quasi-republic of *qaramita* (Carmanthians) in the *hassa* region of eastern Arabia with its capital at Lahsa in Bahrain.

Male slaves could and did become trusted confidants of their powerful masters. Some rose to positions of considerable importance. It was not unusual for high-ranking slaves to own slaves of their own. Arabic slave owners often permitted their slaves to work away from home but required them to remit part of their pay to their master. The second Caliph, the warrior 'Umar ibn al-Khattab, was assassinated by his disgruntled slave, who complained about the proportion of his wage which his master was taking from him, and in so doing probably altered the course of Arabian history, as the Caliphate succession showed.

A penitent Muslim might expiate his sins through manumission, but the demand for slaves still needed to be met. Slave children born to slave parents could not meet that demand, particularly for young females, so they needed to come from elsewhere. Indeed Arab traders had dealt since antiquity in that most emotionally-challenging African commodity – *'abd aswad'* – 'black slaves', predominantly from the Bantu tribes from the coast of East Africa. It has been estimated that about 1,000 African slaves were traded annually up to the end of the sixteenth century with the number increasing fourfold before the British intervened. The enslaved were shipped northwards from the Arabian outpost at Rhapta near Zanzibar, where the language of the coast, *lugha is-sahil* (hence *saw'ahil* – the plural of *sahil*) – was and is Swahili.

White slaves, *raqeeq abyadh*, came principally from the Slav states, from which the word is derived. It has been estimated that Corsairs from the Barbary coast captured over one million European slaves from the sixteenth to eighteenth centuries. There is absolutely no doubt that the capture and subsequent treatment of slaves before they were bought by their masters was reprehensible. For example, castrated slaves were employed to guard the female quarters, but because the Quran forbids mutilation, the 'manufacture' of eunuchs, as Lewis called it, was generally conducted before the slaves entered the Islamic Empire. Some male slaves were militarised. The Ottoman rulers inaugurated a new army (*yeni ceri* – hence 'Janissary') formed from specially selected converted slave boys from the slave quota (*devshirme*) of Christian regions, trained as an elite fighting force. They were originally bound by an oath of celibacy and lived in barracks. However, over time their esprit de corps and code of honour was diluted and the army was eventually abolished in 1826. A few years later, Captain Haines commented that Arabic society in the small coastal town of Marbat to the east of modern-day Salalah comprised about 200 souls, divided into three classes. The upper tier were Arab merchants who had not been born there, the middle class comprised local Gharrah tribesmen, often with *bedu* wives, and the lower class were slaves, 'the females of which are not celebrated for their morals'.

The price demanded for British friendship and protection of Omani commerce was the cessation of its highly profitable Arabic slave trade. The same was true within the Gulf. Despite Shaykh Mohammad Al-Qasimi's alternative view mentioned in Chapter 10, well-documented reports of slave-connected piracy were recorded by Lorimer. He wrote that in 1819, a year before the treaty with the Arab Tribes was signed, 'several Indian women had been brought from Ra's al Khaimah and sold in the Bahrain bazaar as slaves'. Negotiations by a Royal Naval captain succeeded in obtaining 'the liberation of seventeen Indian women who were held in captivity by the Qawasim' at Ra's al Khaimah. These actions diminished Arabian slavery from the 1820s onwards, when a combination of economic and social modifications and international efforts to curb the trade in humans had (so Hourani put it) 'more or less brought an end to domestic slavery by 1914'. It was not abolished formally until as late as 1970 when the new Sultan of Oman, whose father, Said bin Taimur, famously had a slave retinue, followed the example of the Gulf states, Saudi Arabia, and Yemen, which had abolished it eight years earlier. A British report from Aden in 1936 estimated that several thousand men and women were still enslaved in the country. It still persisted after World War Two.

In his *Arabian Sands*, Thesiger noted that 'Arabs have little if any sense of colour-bar; socially they treat a slave, however black, as one of themselves', even though some of them could become 'overbearing and ill-mannered; trading on their master's position' – a trait not uncommon among flag lieutenants in the Royal Navy! He was surprised to find in 1948 that the young Amir of a town on the north-west side of the Empty Quarter was a slave. The town of Dibba, on the border between Oman and the UAE, was also governed by a slave some twenty years later. Thesiger also noted that in the same year, two shipwrecked Arabs were sold to a well-known slave dealer whose caravan of forty-eight captives was bound for a slave market in the Hassa region of Saudi Arabia. He also reported that Baluchis, Persians, and Arabs were sold in another slave market near Buraimi (in the Emirate of Abu Dhabi) for '1,000 to 1,500 rupees, and for a young Negro even more. An Arab or Persian girl was however more valuable than a negress and would fetch as much as 3,000 rupees'.

Most African slaves were shipped to Arabian and Red Sea ports from Zanzibar, which Lewis described as 'a great slave mart'. European slave traders included the French. In 1816 they sent thirty-six of their ships on slaving missions, which included calls at Zanzibar. A contemporary observer noted that when slaves arrived there for sale, 'they are discharged in the same manner as a load of sheep would be, the dead ones thrown overboard to drift down with the tide'. The British Resident (Consul) who had been appointed to Musqat in 1849 was almost immediately transferred to Zanzibar, because as Lorimer put it, Sayyid Sa'id bin Sultan 'generally' resided there. The Sultan oversaw international trade and the local production of cloves and coconuts – commodities serviced by slaves. Oman and Zanzibar became separate Sultanates in 1861 when a British consul was also appointed to Musqat. In the mid-nineteenth century, the then British foreign secretary Lord 'Pumice Stone' Palmerston told the British consul in Zanzibar to 'take every opportunity of impressing on the Arabs that the nations of Europe are destined to put an end to the African slave trade and that Great Britain is the main instrument of Providence for the accomplishment of this purpose'. Slavery was not abolished there formally until 1897, when its Sultan, Hamoud bin Mohammed Al Said, was knighted by Queen Victoria for doing so.

British pressure to suspend the slave trade struck at the very heart of the Arabian economy and society, particularly as it was regarded as being permitted by several Quranic verses and therefore by God. The author of Oman's Department of Information book, published in 1972 to celebrate its second national day following the accession of Sultan Qaboos, wrote that slavery 'in the Arabian context does not have the same sordidness and implication of cruelty as it does in the European tradition'. It noted that slaves were 'family retainers and servants [who] performed the menial tasks' on which society depended. It stated critically that the slave treaties 'may have caused a glow of righteousness in English hearts [but] for Omanis they gave rise to effects which ran counter to the commercial prosperity of the country, and caused much bitterness'.

The estimate of the extent and quantity of slaves taken to Arabian and North African markets varies considerably. Some place it as high as eleven million between the ninth and twentieth centuries, a figure comparable with Hugh Thomas's estimate of those shipped across the Atlantic from the fifteenth century. Some commentators have sugar-coated the treatment of enslaved 'infidels' in Arabia while others insist that the trade, particularly in the conditions of employment of Indian sub-continent labour, continues to this day. It certainly remains a sensitive subject and one best avoided as a visitor to Arabia, but one cannot hide the fact that evidence of Arabia's earlier dependence on slaves still lingers. The manacle rings hammered into the harbour wall at Sur on the sea route from Zanzibar to Musqat were still plainly visible until removed quietly at the turn of this century. I would have preferred it if they had been left in situ as a reminder that individual freedom and the respect for all humanity and their faiths (or lack of them) requires undiminished surveillance.

CHAPTER 19

غ   ghayn
غرب   gharb

West

From our perspective, Polaris appears to revolve in a tiny circle over the North Pole. This makes it a significant marker to us in the West. It is thought to be about four hundred and fifty light years away, so that what we see today left that triple-star system about the time that the first Western conqueror of Arabia, Alfonso De Albuquerque, died near Goa. While Westerners maintain north as their principal point of reference, Arabs have historically faced east towards the rising sun. The western lands behind them are less well understood. 'Sunset' is *gharoob* in Arabic, from *gharb* meaning 'west'. Its close etymological relative, *ghareeb*, means 'strange'. The pronunciation of that guttural-sounding word with its unfamiliar back-of-the-throat 'gh' is equally strange to us in the West.

The ninth-century CE Persian polymath, Mohammed Khwarizmi, considered the Western Franks to be 'filthy, unhygienic and treacherous, given to savagery, sexual licentiousness and warfare'. The Arab historian, Al Masudi, considered Westerners to be 'gross in nature, harsh-mannered and heavy-tongued'. An eleventh-century Muslim judge, writing from Toledo, wrote of 'contemptible pale-skinned and corpulent European Barbarians, closer to beasts than humans, who lacked keenness of understanding and clarity of intelligence and are overcome by ignorance and apathy, lack of discernment and stupidity'. So that summed us up then! Similarly, the West has not always had an entirely favourable view of Arabia. Thanks to Travis Zadeh's masterly account of thirteenth-century Zakariyya Qazwini's *Wonders and Rarities* we learn that in the western imagination

'Islam was tyrannical and oppressive, its adherents superstitious, decadent, childish, ignorant, feminine, deviant and deceptive'. Rudyard Kipling wrote that 'never the twain shall meet', and there are certainly significant differences that separate the Islamic Middle East from the Infidel West, not least in terms of mutual trust and understanding. One is perhaps the manner in which the West approaches those of different cultures. Sir Kinahan Cornwallis, in his introduction to Freya Starks' *A Winter in Arabia*, pointed out that 'the average Englishman is not blessed with an exaggerated sense of imagination in his dealings with other races'. The same might well be applied to a few of the less imaginative representatives of Western governments, companies, and military forces who have interacted with their Arabian counterparts. No less a person than the experienced diplomat Sir Donald Hawley wrote that 'the lack of knowledge of local manners may not only mar a trip to the Middle East but also wreck the chance of doing business and damage the reputation of an individual *and his country*' (my italics).

During a visit by a government minister to Oman in the early 1990s, he informed me that it was my job to sell British weapons to the Omanis. When I reminded him that my remit as a loan service officer was to propose British equipment, but only if it was the most appropriate, he was apoplectically rude, although I am certain that time to reflect in prison after his committal for perjury calmed him down no end. I found this ignorant attitude still prevalent in some officers in the Ministry of Defence in London when I returned regularly to brief deploying ships in the period between the two Gulf Wars. One newly promoted half-colonel referred to Arabs as 'rag heads'. I asked him if he meant the people who had named the stars and reintroduced algebra to the West. Unsurprisingly he had no appropriate response.

Nigel Biggar, in his book *Colonialism*, reminded us that King Faisal I 'and others were not infrequently irritated by the high-handed manner of British officials'. In the *Seven Pillars of Wisdom*, T. E. Lawrence recounts that at a lively debate in 1916 with Feisal (Lawrence's spelling) concerning secret overtures to European governments which had led to a number of Arab leaders being executed by the Turks, the wise Feisal winked at him and explained that 'we are now of necessity tied to the British. We are delighted to be their friends, grateful for their help, expectant of our future profit. But we are not British subjects. We would be more at ease if they were not such disproportionate allies'. These western strangers were welcome but not always entirely trusted. Even Glubb, who lived closely with Arabs, encountered a 'maddening tendency to attribute some treacherous and sinister motive to my most sincere efforts to serve them'. Several of my loan service brother officers have experienced the same sense of mild resentment against them, despite their best efforts to integrate and avoid any form of patronising attitude.

Others who were sensitive to cultural differences were Sir Percy Cox and the intrepid Gertrude Bell, both of whom were much admired and respected for it. Cox, high commissioner and then ambassador in Iraq (1920 to 1923), was considered by the Iraqi politician and scholar, Ali Abdul-Amir Allawi (celebrated author of *Feisal I of Iraq*), to have a knowledge of Arab affair 'probably greater than that of any other person'. King Feisal I, to whom Gertrude Bell was a trusted advisor, died aged just forty-eight in 1933. The rulers of most Arabic states are designated as *emir* ('prince') rather than *malik* ('king'). Bernard Lewis observed that Arabs were generally 'hostile to monarchy'. The title 'king' was nevertheless adopted by the Hashemites, the Al-Saud and, to the amusement of other Gulf states, by the *al-khalifa* ruler of Bahrain, thereby, they hinted, relieving the king of Tonga of the burden of being the monarch with the world's fewest subjects!

The rulers in Oman were either designated *imam* ('spiritual leader') or sultan (from *sulta'* – 'power') and never *malik*. Male members of the royal family are designated *sayyid* ('lord') and addressed as Your Highness. It was during quiet conversations with my boss, Sayyid Shihab bin Tariq Al Said, that I came to appreciate more closely how he viewed the status of his Western employee. During this second stint working for him, I was employed principally for my technical expertise. Although he clearly liked me, I could never offer an opinion unless asked to do so. He also saw me as an informed conduit of how other Omanis saw him and how his nation was regarded by other Gulf states. Even then my responses needed to be couched in courteous and formal terms. I could never, for example, use the word 'you' either in minutes to him or in conversation. It was always 'Your Highness'. For example, should he ask whether I had heard of local disquiet in the country (the Omani press never carried bad news), I would respond by saying, 'I did sense some concern when I travelled to [specified region], Your Highness, but understand that under the wise leadership of His Majesty, Sultan Qaboos, matters are in hand, very much improved by the gracious words that I understand Your Highness may have spoken to my staff from [that region].' To those in the West, such seemingly archaic flattery would seem out of place. In the Arab word that is the norm. A Westerner's failure to follow such practice might seem to be forgiven but will never be forgotten.

Exemplars such as Cox and Bell, Glubb noted, had not only listened to and learnt from their hosts 'but taken pains to acquire their language and understand their customs which informed considerably their generally sound judgements'. Another earlier example was the seventeenth-century special advisor to the Persian army, Sir Robert Shirley. Like his brother before him he had travelled to the court of Shah 'Abbas unofficially to persuade the Shah to abandon trade with the Ottomans in favour of the West. Shirley subsequently delivered a letter to King James 'signifying the Persians' great love and affection to His Majesty … with frank offer of free commerce unto all His Highness' subjects throughout Persia's dominions'. His tactics did not meet with universal approval. The last thing the newly formed East India Company wanted was to lose trading links with its Ottoman clients. The soon-to-be accredited ambassador to the court of the Indian Muslim Mughal emperor, Jehangir, Sir Thomas Roe, said of Shirley that 'as hee is dishonest, soo hee is subtle'. Sir Robert returned to Isfahan empty-handed.

However he remained a trusted advisor to the Mughal court, a precursor to many Englishmen who found favour with their foreign masters while engendering some antagonism at home for no longer being 'one of us'.

Antagonism can dwell in the minds of Arabs, for whom time is no barrier to lingering resentment. One such example of anti-Western feeling concerned flags. Powerful tribal identities were represented *inter alia* by war banners, the latter selected from the colours of red for courage, green for prosperity, white for honesty, and black for solidarity. The *hinawi* and *ghafiri* tribal federations who lived between what is now Abu Dhabi and Ra's al Khaimah had a pure red banner representing the Hashemite dynasty, guardians of the Holy Places descended from Mohammad's daughter, Fatimah. The *qawasim*, part of the *ghafiri* federation had a green, white, and red horizontal tricolour used to distinguish them as a maritime power. With the entirely reasonable aim of supressing 'plunder and piracy by land and sea', the British 'persuaded six of the seven Emirates (Fujairah, lying outside the Gulf, did not at that stage belong to the group) to sign the 1820 General Maritime Treaty. Article 3 of the Treaty required 'the friendly Arabs' to replace their tribal banners with one taken from the Naval Signal book, a red flag within a white border which was known in the British Navy by the title of 'white pierced red'.

Harold Wilson's 1968 announcement that British forces would be withdrawn East of Suez was welcomed warmly by many within the Gulf. Sharjah (swiftly followed by Ajman, Umm al Quwain, and Fujairah) readopted the Qawasim tricolour banner, its Emir, Sultan Muhammad Al-Qasimi, stating that the dignity of the citizens of Sharjah had been restored as they had been 'obliged to salute the flag of the very aggressors [the British] who had removed our own flag, a flag that symbolised the struggle of Al-Qawasim'. His genuinely charming nephew, chair of Sharjah Ports Authority during my time in Dubai, took gentle pleasure in reminding me of this story some twenty-five years after his uncle had made his statement, and did not, he assured me, consider me to be in any way an aggressor. He did however always greet me with a twinkle in his eye and the sobriquet *'marhaba ya muqaddam jasoos'* ('Welcome, O Commander Spy').

***

The two sections of the *al-hajar* mountains, formed from uplifted cretaceous ophiolites which face the Gulf of Oman, are split along the line of the Sumail Gap, which connects the coast to the interior. To the east of the Gap lies *al-hajar ash-sharqiyah* stretching south-easterly towards Sur and Ra's al Hadd. In the opposite direction lies *al-hajar al gharbi*, the western range, which includes Oman's highest point, Jebal Shams, the mountain of the sun, so called because it is the first thing to be lit by the sun's rays soon after sunrise (*shurouq* – from *sharq* – 'East'). Sunset, or *gharoob*, can be observed over the sea from the Musandam Peninsula but not from elsewhere in Oman as the sun dips towards the dunes of the desert or more spectacularly behind the white-coloured crescent-shaped peak of Jebal Misht, an exotic limestone formation which stranded on the Arabian Plate in the later Triassic period. From an evening camp on the mountains to the east, its shark's-fin profile turns progressively more purple as the setting sun sinks below it.

True sunset occurs when the orange lower disk of the sun is half its diameter above a sea horizon. This is because light rays are bent downwards through the earth's atmosphere. That is the time when a mariner can check his compass error by taking a bearing of the sun just before it apparently sets some minutes later. As the last orange drop of the sun sinks into the sea, the *bedu* in the desert will be recounting memories while looking into the embers of the dying fire. If an observer lingers in the desert after sunset, it will not be long before its surface erupts into life. Lie on a dune with a good quality night-sight and observe the emergence of small mammals pursuing supper, with sidewinders pursuing them until the first light of dawn calls the faithful to the *fajr* prayer as the infidels slumber on.

Much of the West's focus on Arabia has been based on commercial opportunities further east and more recently the exploitation and protection of its petrochemical resources. For now, liquified products from Iran's South Pars and Qatar's North Dome gas fields will bolster losses from Russian sources while continuing to power industries in China and the Far East. Taken together, the United States losing its dependence on oil and gas from the Gulf, the carbon-neutral drive in much of Europe, and a possible Chinese-brokered reproachment between the Kingdom of Saudi Arabia and Iran (don't hold your breath), Arabia may look increasingly to the East and become less focused on waning Western influence. Until, that is, there comes a time when oil and gas are no longer necessary commodities to be extracted from the deserts and increasingly salty seas of the Gulf. The demands of Arabia's soft-palmed populations, meanwhile, are unlikely to diminish. Their leaders may well then recall the legacy of those strangers who gave such good service in the past and turn with fond memories to face the setting sun.

CHAPTER 20

| ف | faa' |
| فلوس | faloos |

Money

It is often assumed that the kingdom of Saudi Arabia (KSA) and the Gulf states are fabulously wealthy. Taking the measure of Gross Domestic Product (GDP) in 2023, KSA ranks sixteenth place in the world, or twenty five times less than the USA. By comparison, Israel is ranked twenty-ninth, a little ahead of the UAE in thirty-third place, with Oman trailing at sixty-nine, just ahead of Cuba. Using the alternative measure of Gross National Income per capita, Qatar is in second place behind Singapore with its sometime rival KSA in twenty-third place, just behind the UK. According to Mean Wealth by Adult, the Swiss are the wealthiest, with Qataris and Kuwaitis in twenty-seventh and twenty-eighth place respectively and Saudis being in thirty-seventh place, sandwiched between Latvia and the Czech Republic.

A fourth measure is National Net Wealth or Worth, being a state's total assets less its liabilities. Perhaps surprisingly, in 2023 KSA came just after Iran, with the UAE, that beacon of superficial ostentation, just behind Bangladesh. What differentiates KSA and the petrochemical-rich Gulf states from most other nations is that individual ruling families control the wealth on behalf of their population. Upset that population sufficiently, and history has shown that the ruling family will fall. So imaginative commercial diversification by those ruling families into financial services, maritime and air transport, and tourism, for example, are very positive indicators for the future well-being of their people. But where in the past did financial security come from, and how were goods and services paid for?

Chapter 14 showed that the pearl industry sustained the Gulf economy until petrochemicals became the principal Arabian export after the Second World War. But long before that, it had been European demand for other commodities which had made ship owners, port authorities, camel caravan traders, and the tribes that controlled the overland routes wealthy. The heavily defended eastern boundary of Byzantium's *Praefectus Praetorio per Orientem* ran northwards from the Gulf of Aqaba towards the south-eastern corner of the Black Sea and encompassed both Jerusalem (*Ur-u-Salim* – The City of Peace) and Damascus. But hopes to control the eastern maritime route through the Gulf had been frustrated by the Persian Sasanid Empire with its capital at Ctesiphon near modern-day Baghdad. With the frankincense trade over, the principal precious commodity demanded by the European market was Chinese silk. Cargoes on the western maritime route had to be off-loaded at Aden and carried overland to Mecca and beyond because the Byzantine square-rigged ships found it virtually impossible to sail northwards up the Red Sea against the prevailing wind.

Until the arrival of their European rivals, Arabs also controlled the cinnamon trade. Cinnamon was carried directly across the Indian Ocean to Rhapta on the southeastern African coast by Indonesian mariners to be re-exported by Arab traders to trans-shipment ports on the Arabian and North African mainland. So complete was the Arab monopoly of cinnamon that the Romans believed that the spice originated in Africa rather than the Orient. Within these ports, Arab seafarers and merchants mingled with their Mediterranean, Persian, Indian, and African counterparts and traded in aloes, ambergris, leopard skins, silk, spices, tortoiseshell, and textiles. A number of textile names and terms are Arabic. Examples are cotton (*qutun*), damask – 'from Damascus', gauze (silken cloth from Gaza), mattress (from something thrown down – *matrah* – the name of the port at Musqat), mohair (goat-hair cloth from *khaya'ar* – 'choice'), muslin (from Mosul), and sequin from *sika* – a die for minting or a coin from that process.

The overland silk trade routes had been cut during the third-century CE barbarian invasions. They were re-established and continued after the Muslim conquests and continued to flourish until the decline of the Mongol empires in the fourteenth century. The international silk trade was wrested from Persian control after the Battle of Chaldiran (1514) and passed into Armenian hands. Subsequent embargoes were imposed to prevent further imports of raw Persian silk from diluting the Ottoman monopoly. With the Portuguese star waning in the Gulf, the Dutch (and also the English) were the principal contenders for control of this lucrative commodity. It was reported in 1652 by the French traveller, Jean Baptiste, that the Dutch dealt in silk, the English in pepper and spices and the Indian merchants in calico and indigo. Pepper was easily handled and therefore easily shipped. Spices were not so much a luxury as a necessity, for without them meat could not be preserved or rendered edible. Medieval dishes demanded spices in great quantities. The recipe for venison in broth, taken from the English *Forme of Cury'* cookbook of 1378, calls for pepper and a 'powder-forte of ginger or of cinnamon and mace'. This generated nice profits for the spice traders, the Grossarii, named after an Italian unit of mass, the *peso grosso* or 'great beam', which gives us our word 'grocer'.

Whatever the political situation pertaining, goods and services had to be paid for. After the Arabian Conquests had created a unified market across the Middle East, both Roman Byzantium and Persian silver coinage was in wide circulation, with money-changers in every major souk operating with exchange rates set by Islamic law. Gold coinage, that tangible statement of established power, was introduced to the Muslim world in 696 CE. The name of the coinage, *dinar*, was adapted from the Byzantine system it superseded (*denarius*), but instead of the imperial profile, coins were embossed with *bismillah* – in the name of Allah or God. Each *dinar* was sub-divided into 1000 *fils* and remains the currency in Iraq, Jordan, Bahrain, and Kuwait.

The influx of African gold enabled coinage to be minted in great quantity with the 'Abbasid dinar remaining, as Hourani put it, 'an instrument of exchange for centuries'. He reported that Islamic silver coins had been found in Scandinavia and in the Wychwood Forest north of Oxford, a clear demonstration of the extent of their usage. The silver coinage used by the Sasanid Empire was called the *dirham,* its name a derivation of the Greek coin, the drachma. In Umayyad times one *dinar* was equivalent (theoretically) to 10 *dirham*. Its name is only retained in the UAE, where it is worth 100 *fils,* and in Qatar, where there are 100 *dirham* to one Qatari *rial*. The *rial,* from the Spanish for 'real' (Latin *regalis* meaning 'royal'), is used in Oman, where it is sub-divided into 1000 *baisa*. It also forms the currencies of Saudi Arabia and Yemen. In the former it is sub-divided into 20 *qursh* or 100 *halala* and in the latter into 100 *fils*. Egypt, Syria, and Lebanon use the pound, sub-divided into 100 *piastre*.

The silver 40-millimeter-diameter Maria Theresa thaler, named after the mid-eighteenth century ruler of Austria, was accepted as an international trade coin from 1751 onwards. The word 'thaler' comes from the German word for a particular valley, or *thal,* where silver was mined. It resembled the Spanish dollar, also called *Real de a ocho* – 'piece of eight'. Arabs mistakenly thought the coin came from France so called it *ar-riyal al-fransi* ('French rial'). Unlike Islamic coinage, it carried the image of Maria Theresa on its head and the Habsburg Double Eagle on the reverse. Despite this, it became the standard currency of the Hejaz in Western Saudi Arabia, Yemen, and Oman. It was particularly popular in Red Sea ports, where it has been reported that merchants would not accept any other type of currency. Hard currency did not suit everyone. Coastal tribes, often cut off from trading routes, preferred barter to coinage. For example, when Captain Haines contracted local fishermen near Ra's Sharbithat on the southern Omani coast to procure wood and water for his ship, he offered to pay in Indian crowns, but they demanded coarse blue cloth and rice instead.

At its apogee in the mid-nineteenth century, Omani possessions extended from Dhofar to Ra's Musandam, Bandar Abbas, Jask, and Lengeh in Persia and almost 2000 miles of the eastern

African coast from Zanzibar northwards. At this time, the Omani navy numbered four frigates, four corvettes, two sloops, seven brigs, and twenty armed merchantman. This caused the explorer, Richard Burton, to note that such a fleet entitled its Sultan, Sayyid Sa'id bin Sultan, 'a place amongst civilised powers'. However, the division of Oman into two Sultanates after the death of Sayyid Sa'id in 1856 and the opening of the Suez Canal in 1869 diminished the importance of Zanzibarian trade. The 40,000 Maria Theresa thalers, which the British governor in India, keen to safeguard its trading interests in Oman, ordered Zanzibar to pay to poorer Muscat, fell into arrears. It was finally paid directly from Calcutta as 'the Canning Award', named after its governor-general. The 'award' continued to be paid until its discontinuation as late as 1957, funded after Indian Independence in 1947 from Foreign Office (therefore UK taxpayer) coffers.

And with money came tax. In pre-Islamic times taxes were raised from port and customs dues. After the Arabian Conquests, specific taxes were levied on the three main classes of the Arabian and provincial populations. The faithful (believers) paid *zakat* (from the Arabic 'to purify') as a religious duty and one of the five pillars of Islam. The rate of *zakat* was determined by an individual's wealth based on capital assets and was distributed primarily for the benefit of the poor. Today, the payment of *zakat* is mandatory in Saudi Arabia and Yemen. Government-run voluntary *zakat* schemes operate in Kuwait and the UAE and payment is purely voluntary in Oman. Non-Muslim monotheistic subjects living in conquered lands, the so-called 'Peoples of the Book', or *dhimmi*, originally paid *kharaj* a tax on their agricultural land. In return for state protection and the right to worship, they also paid a poll tax – *jizya*, though neither is now levied in Arabia. The third class, the infidels, if unlucky enough to be captured, paid their tax by being enslaved. While a VAT-equivalent purchase tax was gradually introduced by the Gulf Co-operation Council a few years ago, income tax remains unknown in Arabia. Modern *dhimmi* cannot however escape so easily. They may be obliged to pay tourist taxes for visit visas, a rental tax, and to a large extent, subsidise the utility bills for nationals by an ex-patriate mark-up on their own gas, electricity, and water usage. When my Emirati friends learnt that I, as a serving naval officer, had to pay income tax to the UK government while living in Dubai, they were astonished. 'A very un-Islamic practice, O Stef'n. You should complain!' When I told them that a Married Quarters charge on my villa was also deducted from my naval salary, they simply fell about laughing.

CHAPTER 21

ق   qaaf
قبيلة   qabila

Tribe

I attended a number of spectacular national day parades in Oman, seated as available space dictated among white-gowned dignitaries. On one occasion, my neighbour was an elderly Omani shaykh who, somewhat to my surprise, talked right through the western-composed national anthem. Later I asked him why. He shrugged and said, 'This is your music, not the music of my tribe,' before adding, First comes my family, then my followers, then our tribe, then lastly the Sultan.' Wilfred Thesiger observed that to the Arab, all Westerners come from the same 'tribe'. The idiosyncrasies of a western tribesman like me could be 'accepted, even if they were not understood' and years later 'recalled with a smile'. I expect my sheikhly neighbour later told his family about the strange white-eyed tribesman who sat next to him wearing the Sultan's uniform like fancy dress.

The tribe is the only real concept of a cohesive unit in Arabia. The principal element of each tribe is the three-generation family – grandfather, father, and son. This is reflected to this day in the name of each tribal member. The eldest son would be named after his grandfather. For example, the firstborn son of a man called Rashid of the *al-mahrouqi* tribe, whose own father was called Abdullah, would be named Abdullah bin Rashid bin Abdullah al-Mahrouqi. A large tribe might be subdivided into clans named after strong parts of the body, for example the thighs (*fakhkd*) or skulls (*jama'jam*) of the parent tribe, each of which would be ruled by a *shaykh* or *sayyid* ('lord' or 'prince'). They would in turn swear allegiance to the paramount shaykh of a tribal confederation, the *tamimah*.

Tribes were often named collectively after their first leader, for example the *bani ghassan*, or 'Sons of Ghassan', the tribal federation that ruled north-western Arabia in the sixth century CE. Individual shaykhs were selected by the *tamimah* from members of a particular family or house. This was not necessarily the eldest son but a relative of the old shaykh who possessed the best combination of not only courage and leadership but principally luck (*hadh*). Once selected, tribal members paid the shaykh a tax of fealty in return for protection from other tribes. He had to be generous to his followers through fair distribution of acquired possessions and wealth and woe betide any shaykh who forgot this equitable balance. If another leader came along with an offer of a better lifestyle or purer creed to follow then there was no reason not to change. Allegiance for settled tribes followed the same pattern with senior shaykhs, like my national day companion nominally obeying the regional leader or *wali*. The *wali* would in turn take his orders from the national religious or secular leader, *imam* or sultan. The *imam* would decree what was lawful and prohibit what was unlawful under shari'a law. An *imam* had no standing army and relied on the tribes affiliated to him to provide protection by a loyal band of *'askar* ('troops' – from the verb 'to camp', hence 'soldiers'; 'troops'). He ruled by force or personality from his capital with an appointed *wali* in charge of the major towns under his control. Rulings would be cascaded down to the paramount shaykhs. If these were not agreed, conflict would ensue. Such tribal disagreements have been the scaffolding of the history of Arabia.

Large tribes were themselves federated (*suff*). The *bani hilal* – 'that most famous of all Arab Tribes', as Thesiger called them – was just such a federation. So too were the *aneyzeh*, who summered in Syria and Iraq and wintered in the basalt-strewn Nejd desert (*al-najd*), which lies to the north-west of the ill-defined and variable border of the Empty Quarter. The Nejd was explored famously in the late nineteenth century by Charles M. Doughty. He had followed in the footsteps of Richard Burton, the polyglot translator of the *Arabian Nights*, who had visited

Mecca in disguise in 1853. The Nejd lies to the east of *al-jebel ash-shammar*, the mountain home to the great *ash-shammar* tribal federation whose leaders, *al-rashidi*, combined *bedu* with *haḏari* ('settled') lifestyles near the town of Hail and fought with the Turks against the British in World War One.

The two principal stems of Arabic tribes are the *adnani* (descendants of Abraham's son, Ismail) and the *qahtani* (descendants of the Biblical Joktan). They were touched on in Chapter 3, as were the final stem, the so-called 'extinct Arabs' of pre-history, the *ad* and the *thamud*, whose names are immortalised in the Holy Quran. The aristocrats of the *bedu* were the *ash-shareef* tribes (*sharaf* means 'noble'), pure-in-blood descendants from the patriarchs Abraham, Ishmael, and Qahtan. Thesiger considered that 'the most authentic of the bedu' were the *bani kathir* based in the Hadhramaut. Another of the ancient tribes of Yemen was *al-humum*, described by one commentator as a dwarfish people with protruding jaws. Thesiger was told when discussing illegitimate children (to whom no slur was attached because 'it was not the child's fault') that *al-humum* near Mukalla 'have a whole tribal section composed entirely of bastards'. Captain Haines noted that the educated males of the South Yemeni *al-mahrah* tribe were scrupulously attentive to the tenets of Islam, whereas 'the poorer classes show great indifference to it and are unable to repeat the prescribed forms of prayer'. He considered them to be 'extremely crafty, hardy and bold' with 'skins that are deeply dyed with the indigo from their clothes, which are seldom, if ever, washed'.

Middle-class *bedu* were semi-nomads, *id-dar al-arab*, or Arabdar, who lived part of the year in towns. They were considered to be soft and decadent, although the tougher tent-dwelling *ash-shareef* tribesmen had no difficulty staying with them when they travelled to town to trade! Below then in the social order came *al-hukra* – shepherds who guarded the herds of both *ash-sharaf* and Arabdar. The lowest caste of *bedu* were the *as-sulubba*, despised tinkers and scavengers, possible half-caste descendants of Christian Crusaders. Doughty, ever keen to utilise a fine turn of phrase, 'admired the full-faced shining flesh-beauty of their ragged children'. Palestinians (*filasteenee*), a bellicose and well-disciplined race, are thought to be a settled people of Arab descent with little connection to the Biblical Philistines. They were accomplished metal workers, who came from the Aegean and were therefore not strictly Semitic.

Such was the status of *nasab* (ancestry and ancestral tradition) at the end of the ninth century CE that Arab Christians held status over non-Arab Muslims. Only pure-bred Arabs were considered worthy to yield power. Pure Arabs, whether *dhimmi* (non-Muslims living in an Islamic state) or Muslim, were followed in the pecking order by half-blood Arabs, even ones of royal birth. Below them came non-Arab Muslims. The base of the class pyramid comprised non-Arab non-Muslim people who formed the bulk of the population. Over time this changed. After the Abbasid revolution, when the centre of power had moved from Medina to Damascus and then Baghdad, the 'arab-ness' of the empire became diluted. While Arabs remained the court aristocracy, positions of real power were held by those who found favour with the Caliph – many of whom were Persians and Central Asians. Access to the paramount Shaykh, a long-established Arab right, was now through a non-Arab *wazir* ('minister'; 'secretary'; 'vizier') with their offices known as wizaara ('ministries').

The strongest and most persistent tribes found a settled existence in the central oases near present-day Riyadh, subsequently the base of the House of Al Saud. The weaker tribes, including the *adnani* (later called *nizari*), rebuffed by the inhospitable sands, moved gradually northwards and eastwards towards Syria and Mesopotamia, where they too settled and became sheep and goat farmers. One of these tribes, *al-'ajmaan*, described by one commentator as 'treacherous with strangers', had by the end of the nineteenth century become a formidable fighting force. In the thirteenth century, the *bani abdul-qais* settled near Sharjah and became proficient seamen and pearlers, eventually occupying the coastal areas now known as the Emirates of Fujairah, Ra's al Khaimah, Ajman, and Umm al-Qaywayn. Their maritime power was weakened by a resurgent Oman and a British determination to quell their reported piratical tendencies. They lost control of what is now Abu Dhabi to their rivals the *bani yas*, a nomadic tribe that gradually settled there in the mid-eighteenth century, following what Lorimer described as 'the accidental discovery of water at the site'. Eight hundred members of the *al bu falasah* section of the *bani yas* split from their blood relatives in Abu Dhabi in 1833 and settled on the creek at Dubai where, as Lorimer put it, they 'attained indisputably to the status of a separate principality'. The principal families of the two *al bu falasah* sections of the *bani yas* rule this region today, *al nahyan* in Abu Dhabi and *al-maktoum* in Dubai.

In western Iraq, the *bani khalid* tribal federation grew in dominance, where by the late eighteenth century, with the Portuguese gone, the federation gained pre-eminence at the head of the Gulf. They were direct rivals to the *aneyzeh* federation and forced the *al-amarat* section of the *aneyzeh* to the coast, where the *al-sabah* family developed a secure stronghold near what is now Kuwait. Another section of the *al-amarat*, the *al-khalifah*, became the dominant family in Bahrain. On the eastern side of the Qatar peninsula, the *al-thani* family were by the 1860s controllers of commerce and pearling, a family but not strictly a tribe. In 1934, the head of the sixty-strong *al-thani* told an official of the Anglo-Persian oil company that he had no tribe that he could claim as his own.

The Omani Arabs came from two sources, the first from Yemen as waves of migrating tribesmen from the area around the Marib Dam, which finally burst in the last decades of the sixth century BCE. They were the southern *qahtani* tribes, who became known as *yamani*, led by the *al-hina* tribe. The second major migration from *aneyzeh* stock came progressively from the head of the Gulf, led by the *al-ghafir* tribe. Internal *hinawi/ghafiri* rivalries matched those of their northern *bani yas/qasimi* neighbours. An Omani Department of Information document from 1972 stated that 'still today every child in every tribe knows whether his tribe is *hinawi* or *ghafiri*, and *ghafiri* tribes will not agree to disputes being settled by a judge from a *hinawi* tribe'. No ruler could hope to succeed in Oman unless he had the support of both factions – a balance which the present Sultan from the House of Al Said is only too aware of.

The tribes of Arabia in all their categories – *al-fellaheen* gardeners, artisans, pure *bedu*, guards, mariners, merchants, miners, pearl-fishers, shaykhs, shop-keepers, and weavers – formed the hardy, courteous, and adaptable people who populated their rough parallelogram of land, as Lawrence described it. Early trading routes, both maritime and terrestrial, brought with them the cultural influence of external superpowers and their religions, until that is, a new faith emerged which would change both Arabia and those who dealt with it in perpetuity. And that is the subject of the next chapter.

CHAPTER 22

| ك | kaaf |
| كتاب | kitab |

Book

At the start of the seventh century CE, Christianity was the dominant religion from the head of the Gulf, through the Fertile Crescent, down the Nile to Memphis and beyond. In Persian-controlled territories from east of the Tigris to the River Oxus, Zoroastrianism, an early monotheistic religion, was paramount. Bertram Russell claimed it to be a close competitor to Christianity. In the first century CE, Jews had been expelled from their historic heartland in the second great diaspora but practised their religion as far afield as Spain, Yemen, and Ethiopia. Three powerful and interconnected monotheistic religions – later referred to as 'The Peoples of the Book' (*'ahul al-kitab*) – surrounded a central desert of sun, moon, and totem worshippers. I visited the Sabatean ruins of temples to the sun and moon inscribed with its mirror-written boustrophedon script in Marib in November 2006. Tourists were scarce, so the delighted Yemeni guide welcomed us with literally open, and far from fragrant, arms. He sold me a 2,000-year-old stone arrowhead for a few rials, but I guess he may have fashioned it the previous afternoon. No matter – he was happy, I was happy, and we parted as friends.

Caravans from Marib divided when they reached Mecca, which had been a trading and pilgrimage centre from antiquity. By 600 CE, pagan idols had been banished from Greco-Roman temples but were still being worshipped in Mecca, by then the principal trading centre in western Arabia. Within Mecca stood a cube-shaped building, the *k'abba*, which contained the Black Stone, a meteorite, an object of worship from the earliest times. Pilgrims would circumambulate the cloth-covered *k'abba* seven times counter-clockwise, chanting devotion to the supreme Semitic god (*'allaah*) and over a hundred other deities, before making sacrificial offerings to its standing stone idols. The area around the *k'abba* had been declared *harem* ('a sanctuary') in which inter-tribal vendettas were vetoed.

The eastward camel trains headed for Riyadh and beyond, the north-western trains towards the Euphrates and the northern route to Aila, Memphis, and Petra. Although the frankincense trade had diminished, spices, silks, and other oriental luxuries were carried by dromedary trains northwards, to make the southbound return journey laden with Syrian consumer goods otherwise unavailable in central and southern Arabia. Pilgrims attracted trade, so a great annual fair of tented stalls was held, beneath the shaded canopies of which were displayed enticing goods from Damascus, Palmyra, and Ctesiphon. But change was coming to the status quo in the pre-Muhammadan period referred to as *al-jahiliyya* – 'The Age of Ignorance'.

Other Arab prophets such as Salih, the third Arab prophet who urged monotheism, had tried unsuccessfully to shed light on this ignorance. He was a son of Hud, a descendant of Noah, who targeted the idol-worshipping *thamud* tribe from north of Medina. His tomb (*qabr*) lies in the Hadhramaut, 140 kilometres north of Mukalla. Captain Haines recorded that Salih's fame lingered in the far outposts of Arabia in the mid-nineteenth century, celebrated by a 'few half-starved wretches' eking out a living near the coastal village of Hasik east of Salalah. His tomb, 'once an edifice of some strength and splendour', was by then 'a mere heap of ruins' but had been a place of pilgrimage prior to the time of Mohammed. Haines reported that pilgrims 'approached the last resting place of the departed saint with great reverence, walking slowly round it three times, and frequently inclining their heads so as to press their lips on the tomb'. The final resting places of several of these pre-Muhammadan prophets are dotted about Arabia. That of Salih s also claimed to lie in the gekireat cemetery of Najaf, Iraq, and that of the eponymous long-suffering Prophet, Job (*ayyub* – Hebrew *iyov*, meaning 'uncertain'), is claimed by Turkey, Lebanon, and Oman, the last being in the *jebel qarah* to the west of Salalah. The life of that greatest of all Arab leaders, the final Prophet, (*nabhi*) Muhammad (born 570 CE), has been recorded superbly elsewhere. His name is invariably followed by 'God's blessing and peace be upon him'. His great-grandfather had close links with the *al-kharraz* tribe from Yathrib, now called Medina, 450 kilometres north-east of Mecca. Muhammad escaped from there in 622 CE, an event known as *'al-hijra* – 'The Hegira' – literally 'emigration'. He left after his unequivocal message – abandon idol worship and acknowledge only one Creator – resulted in Muhammad's persecution by his own tribe, the Quraysh, because his preaching struck at the very heart of their livelihood. Their subsequent defeat was told in Chapter 6. He returned to Mecca in 630 as the recognised prophet of all Arabia and wrote to each of the world's known leaders with his spiritual message of social reform. Muhammad's first arrival in Medina was later marked as the start of a new era. New Year's Day, 15/16 July 622, in the year of Muhammad's emigration was celebrated as the first day of the new Islamic calendar – 1 Muharram 0000 al-Hijra (AH), a defining moment in the division between ignorance and enlightenment.

Increasingly aware that Arabia was in a state of moral anarchy, Muhammad went on spiritual retreats to the caves of Mount Hira. It was here that in 610 CE, at the age of about forty, he received his first revelation from God (*'allaah*) through the archangel Gabriel (*jibreel*) who ordered him to 'recite!' (*iqra*). These verses (*ayah*), given in fragments over twenty-three years, were the revelations which collectively formed the Holy Quran – 'The Recital'. Muhammad's message, according to the British author and commentator, Karen Armstrong, 'stressed the continuity of the religious experience of mankind' and the Holy Quran is, to those who believe in it, the authoritative word of God. An astonishing legacy.

According to Russell, the religion of the Prophet 'was a simple monotheism, uncomplicated by the elaborate theology of The

Trinity and the Incarnation', a religion of one God, one Quranic message and one final messenger. The prophecy revealed by Muhammad was not new, but it rejuvenated messages from earlier monotheistic scripture to their faithful readers whom Islam recognised as Peoples of the Book. As such there was no need for them to convert to Islam but of course they could do so if they chose. Armstrong defined Islam as 'the act of existential surrender' which each convert was expected to make to Allah. The Quran carries ninety-nine names for God, often recounted on prayer beads, the vast majority of the names conveying attributes of compassion and forgiveness. In contrast, those who had strayed – the idolaters, the unjust, and the selfish – must be brought back to the right path by a God who is the Avenger, stern in retribution, He who takes away and brings low.

Muhammed was very bright but had had no formal education and was barely literate. His recitations in their lyrical, haunting form were written down by others, often on whatever came to hand – stones, palm leaves, or the discarded cooked shoulder-blades of goats. Mecca had resident professional reciters of poetry (*rawi*), who were contracted to commit each *surah* ('chapter') to memory. The literate and poem-loving second Caliph 'Umar ordered the collection and collation of the 114 chapters, with the longest being recorded first and the shortest last. The chapters are therefore not chronological but rather what Pakistani Professor Akbar S. Ahmed called 'a dialogue between God and humanity – a vibrant outpouring of divine messages'.

'Umar's successor 'Uthman authorised a version of the Quran written in a Kufic script, which the introduction to the Penguin Classics translation noted 'contained no indication of vowels or diacritical points' so that 'variant readings are recognised by Muslims as of equal authority'. All but one of the Quranic chapters open with the formula *bismillah ar-rahman ar-raheem* – 'in the name of Allah, The Beneficent, The Merciful'. I first heard the Quran being recited on Oman State Radio just after the first Gulf War and was struck by its lyrical beauty, just as Thesiger had been by 'the lingering music of the words'. To hear the Holy

Quran recited by a professional *muezzin* is magical, and the words of its message (here from the Penguin translation) have a haunting majesty.

> *God is the light of the heavens and the earth, His light may be compared to a niche that enshrines a lamp, the lamp within a crystal of star-like brilliance. It is lit from a blessed olive tree neither eastern nor western. Its very oil would almost shine forth, though no fire touched it. Light upon light; God guides to his light who He will. God speaks in metaphors to men. God has knowledge of all things. [surah 24:35]*

The original customary actions (*sunna*) of the Prophet, reported by a multitude of traditions (*hadith*), had coalesced by the end of the second century AH to give the community (*ummah*) who followed the *sunna* a common religious identity. Thereafter they were known as *as-sunni*. The four *sunni* schools of jurisprudence agreed on matters of prime importance but differed on matters of detail. They agreed that the behaviour of the *ummah* should be divided into five categories: that which was obligatory, recommended but not obligatory, indifferent, disapproved but not forbidden, and finally that which was prohibited. An *imam* ('one who sets an example') is more than just a prayer leader. Professor Albert Hourani explains that they were 'infallible interpreters of the truth contained in the Quran'. An *imam* would be elected by a council of religious experts – *'ulama*. Knowledge is *'ilm*, and one who is learned is an *'alim*; its plural is *'ulama*.

Islamic law – *shari'a* – was named after Muhammad ibn Idris al-Shafi'i (died 820 CE). The interpretations of *shari'a* by the *'ulama* marked, according to Professor Alfred Guillaume the limit between orthodoxy and heresy. When new subjects arose which had no precedent in *shari'a*, the matter was taken to a juriconsult – *mufti* – for an opinion. His pronouncement – *fatwa* – created the framework on which judgements or individual actions could be based. Süleyman the Magnificent was advised by the chief *mufti* of Constantinople, the so-called *shaykh al-islam*. Bernard Lewis considered *shari'a* – 'this magnificent structure of laws, lovingly elaborated by successive generations of jurists and theologians' – to be one of Arabia's greatest legacies 'and perhaps most fully exemplifies the character and genius of Islamic civilisation'. In my experience, too many Westerners are unaware of that magnificent legacy or chose to be overly selective when making judgements on it. A more open-minded encounter with that 'character and genius' might help to ward off another age of ignorance.

CHAPTER 23

ل   laam
لبان   labaan

Frankincense

The English word 'frankincense' comes from the old French *franc encens* or 'high quality' incense. The Arabic word *labaan* is possibly derived from the radicals which form the Arabic for 'white' (*abyad*) and the old Latin *libanus*, associated with Mount Lebanon on the frankincense trading route. The bark of the frankincense-producing *Boswellia sacra* tree is peeled back to allow the sticky yellow resin to ooze out and gradually solidify before its orange-coloured beads are harvested or gathered up from the ground where they have fallen. The best-quality resin is said to come from the trees nearest the desert. The dark red beads of hardened myrrh resin from the thorny *Commiphora myrrha* shrub are similarly harvested.

Incense and myrrh (Arabic for 'bitter') had been used in religious and ceremonial rites from 2800 BCE onwards. The Egyptians used myrrh when embalming their mummies. The Book of Genesis tells us that the camels of the Ishmaelite traders, to whom Jacob's sons sold Joseph, were carrying 'spicery and balm and myrrh' bound for Egypt. The wise men presented frankincense and myrrh to the infant Jesus, whose crucified body was later wrapped ceremoniously in aloes and myrrh. Frankincense resin is burnt in a *mabkhara* ('censer') in Arabia, often to scent clothes or to welcome guests. In the West it is used in Roman Catholic and High Anglican churches to this day but not in anything like the quantities used in the past. It has been estimated that 700 tonnes of incense were burnt annually in Ur, the legendary Chaldean birthplace of Biblical Abraham. The Romans used vast quantities during ritual sacrifices, and Herod the Great's priests used over 270 kilograms of refined incense in the Holy of Holies in his refurbished temple in Jerusalem.

Demand was therefore immense. The stunted trees which produced these fragrant gums grew only in Somalia and the misty mountains of Dhofar and the Hadhramaut in southern Arabia. The cities which produced and controlled the frankincense trade in these regions became very wealthy. These included the Nabataean stronghold of Petra re-discovered (as he put it) in 1812 by the Swiss-born but Anglophile explorer Burckhardt. In return for safe haven, the rulers of these well-watered cities levied duty on the goods passing through them. The Nabataeans, until their subjugation by Emperor Trajan in 106 CE, were a good example of poacher-turned-gamekeeper. When still nomadic, they had raided the camel caravans (*kafily*) but came to see that a steady income required peace and security. They therefore came to an accommodation with their sometime jealous neighbours, a habit which survives to this day throughout the Gulf.

One such well-watered and ancient city mentioned in Chapter 3 was the Sabean capital Marib, called Mariaba by ancient historians, which lies at the confluence of several *wadi* some 135 kilometres east of Sana'a. It was bounded by a 7-kilometre circumference wall enclosing Hellenistic-influenced architecture which was much admired by the second-century BCE Greek writer Agatharchides. Its chief claim to fame, however, was a huge masonry dam (*sudd* in Arabic) constructed across Wadi Adana from massive masonry blocks bound together with metal clamps. I was aware that a new dam, funded by a grant from the UAE ruler, Shaykh Zayed bin Sultan Al Nahyan, had been constructed in Marib in the 1980s but wanted to see what remained of the Sabean original.

The political situation in 2006 was complex and tourism was significantly curtailed, but thanks to the intervention of my friend, the US ambassador to Yemen, my wife, Annie, and I gained the necessary 'permissions' to join a Yemeni army-protected convoy of vehicles which was scheduled to leave Sana'a one cool November morning bound for Marib. The original permit lacked an essential stamp or signature or something, but after patient negotiations and a telephone call from the ambassador to the minister of tourism, we eventually departed at noon. Our vehicle was guarded, if I can use that word, by a delightful seventeen-ish-year-old Yemeni soldier armed with a Kalashnikov rifle which had not seen cleaning oil for some months. He sat next to our driver and immediately fell asleep with the barrel of his rifle, pointing backwards over his seat, aimed alternately, as the bumpy road dictated, at the roof of the car or my head. Fortunately the three-hour journey passed without significant incident and grateful but slightly sweaty hands were shaken when we dropped him off at the guard post on Marib's dusty outskirts.

Twenty or more centuries earlier, Marib (the ancient Sheba) had become one of the great commercial, cultural, and agricultural centres of Arabia, through which passed the Indo-Mediterranean trade route. The city and its gardens (*bustaan*) needed a reliable supply of water. A dam some 300 metres long and 35 metres in height, topped by houses, constrained a mountain-reflecting lake which ran back along the *wadi* for over 4 kilometres. To the south, a wooden sluice gate, contained within interlocking rectangular masonry blocks, controlled the outflow from the huge reservoir into irrigation channels which snaked distantly away to transform the arid terrain into lush gardens. Protected by outriders, trains of frankincense-bearing camels, hundreds of them, moved through the gardens towards the curling smoke fires outside Marib's watch-towered walls to pay the excise duty before continuing northwards to Mecca, Egypt, and Damascus. These biannual caravan trains carried not just goods but gossip, news, and ideas. It was not difficult to reimagine the spectacle as I stood on the still-standing walls of the sluice gate all those centuries later. There were no other tourists, but we were joined by three Yemeni teenagers with long handsome faces, one of them sporting an Everton football jersey. Which team did I support, another asked in very guttural Arabic. 'Arsenal,' I replied and received a pitying look in return.

The Author standing above the southern sluice gate of Marib Dam – 2006

The ancient Marib needed pity too. The good times were not to last. *Surah* 34 of the Quran records that the 'natives of Sheba' were told to *'Eat of what your Lord has given you and render thanks to Him. Pleasant is your land and forgiving is your Lord. But they gave no heed. So We let loose upon them the waters of the dam and replaced their gardens with others bearing bitter fruit, tamarisks and a few nettle shrubs'.* More prosaically, the Sabaean rulers and their Himyarite successors had failed to maintain adequately their greatest asset, which silted up and burst in about 450 CE. Legend has it that Dhareefa, the wife of the ruler's rival, dreamt that rats with iron teeth had gnawed at the bonds holding the dam together. Her Cassandraic warning, however, went unheeded by the ruler and the flood caused by the dam's collapse was catastrophic. Marib was abandoned gradually in favour of Sana'a, and its once-thriving conurbation crumbled into a dusty and sparsely populated cluster of villages. Her warning may not have been far off the mark, as later archaeological examinations revealed that large gopher-like rodents had burrowed under the dam to such an extent that it was undermined critically. Whatever the cause, the relevance of Marib had already waned as the demand for ceremonial frankincense diminished once Byzantium Constantinople had embraced Christianity. The frankincense trade was revitalised as an export to the Chinese market in the twelfth century, where thirteen classes of *ju-hiang* ('incense') harvested from 'the depths of the remotest mountain valleys were valued for their aromatic and medicinal purposes. Marco Polo visited the Dhofar region towards the end of the thirteenth century CE and reported that the 'white incense trees ... are like small fir trees [which] are notched with a knife in several places and from these notches the incense is exuded'. Exports eastwards continued in subsequent centuries. In 1835, Captain Haines considered that frankincense and gum-arabic exports from the ports near present-day Salalah could be expanded considerably, the trees 'being exceedingly numerous on the mountain declivities and in the valleys inland'. He noted that the exported quantity of these commodities amounted to 3,000 to 10,000 maunds, a maund being 100 Troy pounds or about 37 kilograms. Incidentally, in the Ottoman empire this traditional unit of weight, often in the form of a carved stone, was called a batman.

S. B. Miles visited Marbat fifty years later and reported that Indian merchants (Khojas from the West Indian state of Gujarat) traded 'rice, cloth and metal-ware' for three varieties of frankincense collected by local *bedu*, the best called 'nejdi', meaning 'from close to the desert'. In one of his university vacations to Oman, my younger son and I clambered up a slope to the west of Salalah studded with hundreds of *Boswellia sacra* trees to gather a sample of solidified resin for him to burn on his return to the UK. A fist-sized blackened copper pot filled with Omani frankincense sits on the shelf over the fireplace in my study. A few beads placed on the top of the wood-burning stove below it fills the room with its evocative scent, and powerful memories of Oman and the Marib dam come flooding back to enliven even the dullest English day.

CHAPTER 24

م   meem
منارة   min'ara

Lighthouse

The Arabic word for fire is *n'ar*. A 'place of fire' (or 'light') is *min'ara*, which also gives its name to the minaret, the tower from which the muezzin calls the faithful to prayer. The first minarets were constructed in the ninth century CE, but *min'ara* predated these by some three thousand years. Beacon fires had been maintained by ancient Egyptian priests. Fire beacons – the earliest aids to navigation – to guide mariners home had been lit at the ancient port of Kuntasi in the Indus Valley in 2000 BCE. The Greek poet, Lesches, wrote of a lighthouse at Cape Inchisari in circa 660 BCE. Alexander the Great's admiral, Nearchus, reported fire beacons burning on the mountains bordering the Strait of Hormuz forty years before Ptolemy II ordered the construction of that most famous early lighthouse, the Pharos of Alexandria in 284 BCE. Its 110-metre tiered tower carried a polished mirror to reflect the sun by day and a fire beacon by night, just as fire beacons in the sand seas of the Iraqi desert had guided camel trains across its featureless wastes.

Lighthouses, like minarets, are symbols of status, safety, and security and have inspired people from the earliest times. I was lucky enough to commission the construction of one in Oman in 2006, and three major light beacons four years later. One of the latter was on Qibliyyah Island in the Halaniyyaat group, which I had first visited in 1995, as explained in Chapter 14. After I left Oman for the final time, I assisted dozens of maritime nations to meet the standards for the implementation and maintenance of modern aids to navigation (AtoN) during my penultimate career working for the Paris-based International Association of Marine Aids to Navigation and Lighthouse Authorities (IALA).

Arabs may sometimes find the West strange but are just as often keen to adopt best Western practice when it might benefit their international standing. I found this to be particularly so in the maritime field, where the production of their own charts and other practices to improve the safety of navigation in their waters would attract international shipping and with it international trade. The same is of course true of airports and national airlines, each one vying with the others to be considered the most attractive. Just look at the global extent of Dubai Ports Authority and the image and reach of Emirates and Qatar Airways. My contribution to Oman's hydrographic and cartographic capability has been touched on elsewhere, as has my return to Oman to run their private aids to navigation company, AMNAS, and it was in that capacity that Ra's Raysut lighthouse above the port of Salalah was constructed. Its story is told later, but the first lighthouse in Oman had been constructed 600 NM (1,115km) to the nor-nor-east almost a century earlier.

As Nearchus and other ancient mariners recognised, the entrance to the Gulf from the Sea of Oman is not easy to find. The 'Committee of Enquiry on Lighting and Buoying of the Gulf' which met in 1909 recognised that a major light should be established to guide vessels through the Strait of Hormuz. Given the curvature of the earth, a lighthouse needs to be placed at a high elevation above sea level so that it can be seen far over the horizon. If one is say 1.5 metres tall and stands on the highwater line of a beach at 2 metres above Mean Sea Level (MSL), then the horizon will be about 3.8 NM (7 Km) away. For the beam of a lighthouse with a nominal range of 20NM to reach the eye a watchkeeper on the bridge of a medium-sized vessel, the light would need to be about 35 metres above MSL.

One of the islands lying about 10 miles off Ra's Musandam fitted the bill precisely. European seafarers called the two wedge-shaped outer islands Great and Little Quoin after the quoin, or wedge, which was used to elevate ship-borne cannons. The shihuh tribe living in the Musandam named the two outer islands mumar and didamar – 'mother' and 'daughter'. Didamar, being conveniently flat-topped, provided an ideal site for a lighthouse which was operational by 1914, the cast-steel structure having been pre-fabricated in the UK before being shipped to Oman. This was no easy task. Strong tidal flows made securing a vessel alongside the rocks beneath the sheerlegs used to hoist its components up the cliff very difficult. Sadly a number of construction workers died during the construction, two of them laid to rest in the Christian cemetery in a bay just to the south of Musqat.

The giant rotating optic comprising a brass cage holding glass prisms was manufactured by the Chance Brothers using the 'Fresnel' principle to focus the light beam. It was lit initially by kerosene lamps and gave two intense white flashes of light every ten seconds. This 'characteristic' gave the light a unique identity which told mariners that they were in sight of the entrance to the Gulf, where Didamar was, and how to navigate past it with safety. The clockwork mechanism driving the lantern's rotation required rewinding every six hours by a team of seven watch-keepers. Responsibility for its operation was transferred from the Indian Marine Service to the Persian Gulf Lighting Service in 1951, later renamed the Middle East Navigation Aids Service (MENAS), which automated the light in the 1980s. Ownership transferred to AMNAS in 2003, which fully refurbished it three years later. The light was upgraded to a modern rotating beacon with a 23 NM range, and its operation could be monitored remotely in the AMNAS head office in Musqat.

I spent a week on the island to oversee this project. This included the decanting and storage of the mercury from the frictionless bearing which was described in Chapter 9. My boss, the chairman of AMNAS, was keen to preserve the historical artefacts, including the giant optic, which it was hoped would later form the centrepiece of a new maritime museum in the capital. Wooden crates were constructed to store the bubble-wrapped brass and glass items safely. The metal components were held in place by brass screws and linen washers dipped in linseed oil. After ninety-two years the screws could be removed without force, releasing each component and in doing so revealing their uniquely engraved serial numbers. I contemplated this example of magnificent British engineering at the end of each day as I searched for a weak mobile phone signal standing on the edge of the highest cliff with thirty or more bull sharks circulating ominously 60 metres below me.

The formation of AMNAS came about because the historic presence of MENAS owning four lighthouses and several other AtoN in Oman was, to put it politely, irksome to opinion formers, including my boss. HH Sayyid Shihab approached His Majesty Sultan Qaboos in the late 1990s and proposed that Oman should establish its own AtoN service company rather than relying on MENAS, whose revenues from international shipping, which paid for the AtoN, did not reach Omani coffers. Funding for the provision of maritime services is either provided by the state or by a levy placed on the users of such services. As mentioned in Chapter 13, the delivery of an AtoN service must comply with the international standards and specifications laid down by IALA and approved by the International Maritime Organization. And strict standards cost money. When UNCLOS 82 became international law, vessels on innocent passage which did not make a port call could not be charged for AtoN services. Charges called light or navigational dues (navdues) were therefore paid voluntarily to MENAS by international shipping, which recognised the value of the excellent service provided.

HH knew what the existing AtoN service for vessels calling at the three main Omani ports of Salalah, Musqat, and Mina Fahl (the oil export terminal) was inadequate. With a new port at Sohar under construction and others planned, an IALA-compliant AtoN service would need to be funded properly through legally enforced navdues. A royal decree was published in 2003 which granted AMNAS the exclusive right to operate and maintain all AtoN in Omani waters under a concession agreement with the government. The scale of charges was set and the world's first wholly commercial AtoN provider commenced operations. But all was not well. Owners of container ships calling at Salalah refused to pay. Maintenance and repair of the existing sixty-six

AtoN, ranging from small harbour buoys to major lighthouses, had not been carried out due to lack of expertise, although there were plans for AMNAS to sub-contract MENAS to conduct an annual maintenance visit to service the more important AtoN. The government was far from happy.

In late 2004, two years after I had retired from the navy, my wife and I had returned from an extended holiday in South America. Among the few messages on our answering machine was one from the office of Sayyid Shihab which said simply, 'His Highness wonders what you are doing these days?' The following March I was back in Oman as the AMNAS troubleshooter (subsequently general manager), with tasks which included recovering the unpaid navdues, which by then totalled some 600,000 Omani rials or about £960,000. Only about half the existing AtoN were operational and the one semi-trained technician had recently resigned. But within three months I had found an ex-Oman Navy office manager and had recruited and trained three Omani technicians to get the lights working.

Part of their selection process was to determine whether they could handle heights and could swim. The first was straightforward, as there was a handy lattice mast close to the office. The other was less so, because two of them had never tried swimming before. So we all donned lifejackets, went for a boat ride, and jumped in. Despite some initial spluttering, all proved to be just fine, and we struck out for the shore some 200 metres distant. Each was provided with a comprehensive toolkit, safety equipment, and smart blue uniforms. With the AtoN operational, the international ship owners, reminded courteously of their legal obligation to pay, reluctantly agreed. One minor Salalah-based shipping agent representing small vessels refused to follow suit, so we paid him a visit. I started to assess what assets he had in his office that we might remove in lieu of payment. He called the police. This was not his wisest move, because once shown a copy of the royal decree, the officer ordered that the outstanding invoices should be paid on the spot. Hands were then shaken and coffee shared, with the agent still muttering that I was worse than a Somali pirate.

Two years later AMNAS had a staff of eleven. All of them apart from me were Omani nationals and they rose magnificently to the occasion. The number of AtoN had increased to over a hundred – all of them operated and maintained to full international standards. The initial three technicians were promoted to junior managerial roles identified by white overalls. I wore white overalls too on deployment, made-to-measure as mentioned in Chapter 8. By the time I turned over to my Omani general manager in 2012, AMNAS owned and operated 174 AtoN and maintained another ninety under contract. Since then, the company has expanded further and remains a beacon of excellence in the Arab world. The training courses and simple risk management system developed for the staff were adopted by IALA and subsequently formalised by the IALA academy for delivery worldwide, an Arabian legacy acknowledged not only by the International Maritime Organization but by countries as widely separated as Finland and Fiji.

The provision of effective AtoN must be based on the degree of risk to safe navigation. The greater the risk, the more AtoN must be provided. The strategically located port of Salalah expanded dramatically in the first decade of this century to handle the world's largest container ships. Force six to eight winds raise significant waves in their approach during the south-west monsoon (khareef) season. Floating AtoN (buoys, etcetera) are subject to extremes of weather so must be designed to cope with such extremes and remain operational to keep mariners safe. Buoys are also famous bird magnets, and their droppings foul the lanterns and the solar panels which power them. Coiled spring wires and strips of plastic 'flock-off' bird spikes deter those pesky contaminators most effectively. In the warm waters of Arabia, buoys also attract weeds, molluscs (which literally eat into the steel hull), crabs, and tiny fish. These in turn attract their larger cousins and therefore of course local fishermen, who find buoys very handy mooring points and also, annoyingly, a handy source of batteries with which to start their outboard motors. The AMNAS team developed a very effective briefing scheme to educate local communities, starting with the Shaykh, on the importance of these aids to safe navigation and the preservation of life at sea. This included inviting the Shaykh to adopt and protect a buoy as part of his tribe!

As recounted in Chapter 13, a red-and-white-striped eight-tonne 'safe water' buoy fitted with an 8 NM marine lantern marking the outer limit of the dredged channel must stay 'on station' no matter what nature throws at it. But should satellite navigation systems fail or smaller vessels require guidance to safety, a longer-range lantern would be needed at sufficient height above sea level to shine a focused beam of light way beyond the horizon. A new lighthouse above Salalah was deemed to be essential, and given that fact that the city houses a royal palace, it was determined that its appearance should impress the local population by reflecting the maritime heritage and culture of Oman.

The mottled dark-and-light limestone cliffs of Ra's Raysut rise 30 metres above the long outer breakwater arm of the port. The successful lighthouse design positioned reassuringly above it comprised a 9-metre high two-tiered tapered reinforced-concrete tower incorporating Islamic architectural features. The upper tier was brilliant white, the lower tier to be clad in polished grey local stone. It would be topped with a domed lantern house surrounded by a stainless-steel balcony and fitted with a modern rotating 20 NM range light, its curved rear wall designed to prevent the eyes of Salalah's inhabitants from being blinded at night! The dome would be surmounted by a brass weathervane. To enhance its conspicuity, especially for small vessels and locals driving past at night, its walls would be floodlit from lights set into the surrounding plinth. The construction started in November 2007 and the lighthouse, the first to be constructed in Arabia for decades, became operational two years later. New architecturally splendid lighthouses are rare. To have commissioned min'ara ar-raas raysut to enhance the safety of navigation for all vessels using or passing the port was a highlight of my time managing AMNAS. Hopefully the loom of its light will reassure mariners and keep them safe long after I have been forgotten.

Mina Raysut Lighthouse, Salalah – 2009

CHAPTER 25

ن   noon
نجم   najm

Star

During my first term at Britannia Royal Naval College Dartmouth in 1967, we were introduced to the delights of astronomical, or celestial, navigation. Satellite-derived position at sea was in its infancy, so the use of the sextant to measure the altitude of planets and stars and then derive position out of sight of land by using astronomical tables was one of the essential competencies required by any aspiring seaman officer. Sadly we were taught the theory of this historic skill, perfected since the time of Newton by Nelson, Cook, Beaufort, and Fitzroy, by one the most boring people it has been my lasting displeasure to encounter. He hectored rather than lectured and demonstrated little if any imagination. Words like Alpheratz, Mirfak and Spica, almanac, azimuth, and zenith tumbled from his lips with not a hint of their almost two-thousand-year-old historical legacy. Fortunately, other much more worthy naval officers gave me a basic understanding of the derivation of these words.

This was especially so when *HMS Beagle*, my first appointment as a junior hydrographic surveyor, was tasked in early 1972 with charting Mahe Atoll in the Maldives, some six hundred years after Ibn Battuta had called there en route to India. The survey of the shallow reef-filled lagoon was required prior to a visit by Her Majesty the Queen, embarked on in the Royal Yacht Britannia. The existing nineteenth-century chart was referred to no known datum. It carried such warnings as 'this island is deemed not to exist'. It was therefore necessary, in those pre-satellite-navigation days, to construct a geodetic pillar, like the ones erected by the Ordnance Survey in the UK, in a clearing on one of the islands and determine its position on earth using as precisely a timed set of astronomical observations as it was possible to achieve. While my mentor, Commander Richard Campbell, waited in that zero-light-polluted night for his preselected stars to be observed in the pillar-mounted astrolabe, he fired my imagination by telling me about early Arab navigation and how over a hundred of the stars had got their names, including that magnificent literally overarching feature, *id-darb at-tab'aana* – 'The Milky Road' (or 'Way').

A little over one and a half thousand years before Galileo was held under house arrest by the Inquisition for his heliocentric beliefs, Claudius Ptolemy had compiled his astonishing astronomical masterwork *The Almagest* (from the Arabic *al-majisti*), later called *The Great Treatise*. This included a tabulated star catalogue, or almanac (a pseudo-arabic word with its prefix 'al'), of just over a thousand celestial bodies grouped into forty-eight constellations. The original Greek text was translated first into Arabic and then later, in the twelfth century, into Latin. The Arabic names of Ptolemaic stars, often described by their position within a human or animal-named constellation, were adopted by the West after the Latin translation became widely circulated. For example, Deneb, in the Greek constellation Cygnus ('the swan') came from *dhanab ad-dajajah* – 'the tail of the hen' (no swans in Arabia except as migratory vagrants!).

Many of these names start with or contain the Arabic definite article 'al' without its 'sun-sign' pronunciation. Examples are Aldebaran (*ad-dabar'aan*), 'The Follower', and Fomalhaut (*fam al-hout*), 'The Mouth of the Whale'. Poor Aldebaran perpetually follows his lover, Thuraya (*al-thuray'aa* – the name Arabs gave to the prominent Pleiades star cluster), through the circulating night sky, never able to embrace her. The name of the red supergiant in Orion, Betelgeuse, is derived from (*al-*) *yad al-jowza* – 'the hand of the Central One'. The second-brightest star in Ursa Major, Dubhe, one of the pointers to Polaris, is named after the back (*kahil*) of the bear (*ud-dubb*). The other pointer, Merak, is named after the loins (*al-mar'aaq*) of the same bear.

Seasonal changes signifying, for example, the onset of autumnal rains, were signalled to Arab observers by the setting of bright stars at dawn. Two were named after birds of prey (*an-nisr'aan*). Vega, the brightest star in the Constellation of Lyra, was named after the falling eagle, or vulture (*an-nisr al-waqi*), and its cousin, *an-nisr at-t'aair* – 'the flying eagle', in the Constellation Aquila, gave us the twelfth-brightest star in the night sky, Altair. These star names, together with others, such as Rasalhague (*raas al-ḥawwa* – 'head of the snake man') and the blue supergiant, Rigel (*rajul*, meaning 'leg'), diagonally across Orion's Belt from Betelgeuse, are yet more examples of Arabia's lasting heritage to all mariners and stargazers. Their relevance is shown in the Quranic *surah* 6:97: 'It was He that created for you the stars, so that they may guide you in the darkness of land and sea', a reminder that terrestrial navigation across the featureless sands was equally as important as its maritime version.

Polaris, which the Arabs called *al-jady* ('young goat' or 'kid') rotates in a tiny arc around the geographic North Pole (Chapter 19). Its elevation above the horizon is therefore almost the same as the latitude of the observer. The head of the Gulf has a latitude of about 30°N, that of Ras al Hadd, 22°N, and the Bab al Mandeb 12°N. This meant that Polaris was never too far above the horizon for early Arab mariners to determine their latitude, an essential element in maritime navigation. Bertrand Russell noted that the Arabs did not acquire their detailed knowledge of celestial navigation until the eighth century CE. The requirement for a greater understanding of astronomical phenomena was driven in part by the need to know the direction of Mecca and the times of sunrise and sunset for fasting during Ramadhan. This led to the tenth-century compilation of *The Book of Fixed Stars* – *kitab suwar al-kaw'akib* (the final word being the plural of *kukab*, another term meaning 'star').

The name of the brightest star in Ursa Minor, Kochab, comes from the same root. Its circumpolar position in the northern night sky made it, like Polaris, a reliable cornerstone of navigation from at least 1500 BCE. The astonishingly comprehensive

The Book of Fixed Stars by the remarkable Persian astronomer, Abdul-Rahman al-Sufi, was based on Ptolemy's catalogue with star coordinates updated to the year 964. The 'little cloud' – *as-sahabat as-sighirah*, the Arabic name for the smudge of the Andromeda Galaxy, was included for the first time in al-Sufi's masterpiece, observed and recorded six hundred and fifty years before the first telescope was invented.

Arab mariners had had contact with their Indian counterparts long before the Islamic era began. Some cross-pollination of navigational competency must therefore have occurred. What is certain is that 'latitude sailing' – holding an east/west course which maintained a fixed altitude of Polaris above the horizon or knowing the rate of change of latitude when sailing north/south, was known to Arab mariners from the earliest times. Prominent landmarks such as Split Rock, mentioned in Chapter 2, and marine phenomena such as the humpback whale population off Masirah and concentrations of sea snakes off the Indian coast, provided signs and indications (*'aashar'aat*) of geographical position. These were recorded in early Arabian navigation manuals called *rahmani*.

There are of course 90° between the horizon and the zenith, the latter derived from *as-samat ar-raas* ('the direction of the head'), the opposite of which is 'nadir', from another Arabic word – *nadheer* – meaning 'counterpart'. An outstretched arm pointing towards the horizon with the thumb uppermost and little finger extended downwards subtends an angle close to 15° no matter how long your arms are. Pivot the hand six times from the horizon and your thumb will be at your zenith. Try it. If you want proof, stand in front of a mirror with your arm outstretched and get your partner, or other kind soul, to mark two dots on the mirror and then measure the distance (d) from the mirror to your eye. Measure the distance between the dots (s), then the angle subtended by your outstretch arm (θ) can be calculated using the tangent rule ($\tan^{-1}\theta = s/d$).

Arabian navigators used not only the outstretched arm but also the width of one or more outstretched fingers (*'asb'aa* is 'finger' in

Arabic). The angle subtended by one finger – one *'asb'aa* – is approximately 1.6°. If a vessel sailed due north at, say, 4 knots, then it would travel 96 NM in a day. Polaris would then be 1.6° higher above the horizon (1° higher = 60NM, so 1.6° higher = 96NM). The distance sailed in three hours was called a *zam* – an eighth of an *'asb'aa*. Arab mariners gained knowledge of the magnetic properties of the lodestone from the Chinese in the eleventh century and used it to fashion a primitive magnetic compass, the use of which was exported to the Mediterranean by Arab mariners in the thirteenth century. The bearing, or azimuth (from the Arabic word *as-samat* – 'the way'), of a destination derived from a compass heading was verified from the rising and setting properties of known stars listed in the *rahmani*. Position at sea out of sight of land could then be estimated using dead reckoning using the course steered and the speed of the vessel through the water.

Measuring the altitude of Polaris or another star linked to Polaris, using tables in the *rahmani*, could be obtained with some accuracy using a small rectangular measuring device – the *kamal* (literally the Arabic for 'perfection') – made from *khashab* ('wood') or horn. A thin knotted cord passed through a hole in the centre of the *kamal*, the knots indicating a certain number of *'asb'aa*. The navigator would grip one end of the cord in his teeth, align the lower edge of the *kamal* with the horizon and keep the cord tight with the other hand. The *kamal* would be adjusted so that its top edge just eclipsed the star being observed. The number of knots between the observer's teeth and the *kamal* would give the altitude of the star in *'asb'aa* (and therefore latitude if using Polaris) or when observing another bright star, latitude from information held in the *rahmani*. The cords of some *kamal* were knotted with the known latitudes of certain ports so that the navigator could assess how far north or south of an intended port of call his vessel was. The accurate latitude of ports and havens was determined ashore using astronomical measurements with *al-'idadah* (an 'alidad' or 'alidade') and perfected later using a planispheric astrolabe. This knowledge made navigation an Arabic speciality.

One famous *mu'allim* ('sea pilot'), Shihab al-Din Ahmed bin Majid, gathered his navigational and pilotage information together in verse form in his 1490 CE collection, *kitab al-fawa'id fi usul al-bahr wa'l-qawa'id* – (the) *Book of Profitable Things Concerning the First Principles and Rules of Navigation* – which focused on the two pivotal landfalls of Ra's al Hadd and Shihr on the Hadhramaut coast. It is thought by some that Vasco da Gama was so impressed by Ahmed's expertise that he contracted him to be his pilot on his voyage of discovery to the Indian coast. This might not have been the case, but his name and that of his successor, Sulaiman al-Mahri, who wrote his own navigation textbook in 1511, live on in Arabia just as the names of Cook and Beaufort do in the West.

The presence of Polaris featured heavily during OPERATION HARLING in 1985 (Chapter 15). I was equipped with a geodetic satellite navigation receiver to fix my position on the coast on either side of the Gulf of Suez. These positions were required so that the British minehunters could fix themselves accurately using precise land-based navigation beacons while searching with their sonars for Gaddafi's influence mines. One selected site was at the fringe of the Sinai near Ra's Sedr. The Egyptian commodore had given approval for one of the minehunters to land me, my assistant, and our equipment over the beach. Sailors waded ashore bearing loads on their heads as I set up the campsite and started initial observations. An army truck was scheduled to collect us three days later. As so often happens in even well-administered countries, information from the central authority does not always trickle down to its outposts. Imagine the surprise then of a two-man army patrol which encountered two desert-camouflaged Brits tucking into their twenty-four-hour ration pack meal, which had just been cooked over a driftwood fire.

The initial confusion, with some waiving of rifles, dissipated once a young and highly effective Egyptian infantry lieutenant, summoned by a garbled radio message, arrived. Hands were shaken and sweet tea was served until a confirmatory signal was received from army headquarters that we were not spies after all. The thing which swung it firmly in our favour was not smiles and reassurances but the rich canned fruit pudding and custard which we offered them from our ration packs. Seemingly this was ambrosia personified. Future patrols seemed to grow in size. Luckily we had double the number of packs required for a two-night stay and no one returned disappointed.

If supplies of English pudding were not a problem, anti-personnel mines laid during the Arab–Israeli conflicts just over a decade earlier most certainly were. The sites for these battery-powered shore transmitters needed to be clear of the minefields as well as high enough above the high-water mark to be protected from the sea. This required taking a range and bearing from my satellite-derived position to each beacon across the mined areas. Range was a straightforward matter using an infrared measuring device fitted to my theodolite. With no fixed points within sight, the bearing had to come from astronomical observations. And there, some 29° above my head, shone the steady light from Polaris. With tabulated corrections from the *Nautical Almanac*, the true azimuth of the beacon from my position could be calculated and its coordinates simply derived to be passed to the minehunters. This combination of cake, celestial, terrestrial, and satellite navigation enabled the Gulf of Suez to be cleared so that international shipping could once again flow through the Suez Canal. The kid, *al-jady*, had saved the day!

CHAPTER 26

ه   haa'
هلال   hilaal

New Moon

During the early rule of the second Islamic khalif, the tall, impetuous Umar ibn al-Khattab, his Arab forces had advanced successfully into Syria but were threatened by the Sassanid Persian army based on the eastern bank of the River Euphrates. They had lost the 'Battle of the Bridge' in October 634, their commander Abu Ubaid bin Masud having been crushed to death under the feet of a Persian elephant. Thirteen months later, in the year the Irish monk, St Aidan, founded Lindisfarne monastery to help convert the heathen Anglo-Saxons, Arab forces, reinforced by tribes who had earlier been classified as apostates, faced the Persians again at the battle of Buwaib in which they were victorious. Two of the reinforcing tribes from Northern Syria, the Bani Namir and Taghlib, had previously embraced Christianity but elected to join their Muslim brothers against a common enemy. The Christian shaykh of the Bani Namir died in the battle. His name was Anis bin Hilal. Hilal is a common boy's name in Arabia and has been for millennia. Many will recognise the name Al-Hilal as the Saudi Arabian football club which offered Paris Saint-Germain an astonishing £259 million in mid-2023 for the French striker, Kylian Mbappe, part of the kingdom's strategy to bolster its international position by bankrolling world sport. For us though, *hilaal* simply means 'new moon'.

Unlike the big aspirated 'haa' sound of the letter ح (Chapter 6), haa' starts with the softer letter ه, shaped like a small curled-up animal, or more fancifully Coleridge's 'new moon with the old moon in her arms'. His poem *Dejection* starts, 'Late, late yestreen I saw the new moon …', but it could not have been too late, because the sliver of the silver crescent of the new moon is just briefly visible above the western horizon after sunset. This follows the moon being in syzygy with the sun some seventeen hours earlier. This double-gravitational pull of heavenly bodies raises higher spring tides on earth just after a new moon (and again of course with a full moon), making the Islamic calendar very convenient for tidal predictions.

Predictions of the future, so common in the West, are however never taken for granted in Arabia. These include basing the appearance of a new moon on purely astronomical calculations, for it is believed that only God knows what is to come. My very worthy administration manager at AMNAS, for example, would never consider starting any car journey without first intoning '*bismillahi*' – 'In God's name'. So one is advised to say that 'hopefully' an event such as a moon sighting will occur by prefacing or closing one's comment with *insha-allah* ('God willing').

I well remember attending a meeting between my boss, the commander of the Royal Navy of Oman, and an equal-ranked visiting British rear admiral when his visitor said on departure, 'See you at the reception on board this evening, Your Highness.'

Sayyid Shihab simply added '*insha-allah* – I hope so'. I explained this cultural difference to the young admiral in my car during our way back to his flagship in Mina Qaboos, for which he was both interested and grateful. When he was later Commander-in-Chief Fleet (and my boss) he remembered the event and told me that the judicious use of *insha-allah* during subsequent visits to Gulf countries had been warmly received. I hope that it also came in handy when he was elevated to the Peerage and given ministerial rank, where he might murmur that phrase following a meeting with an unwavering Member of Cabinet whose firm views of the certain outcome of his or her policy in practice came to naught.

The only reliable celestial calendar to many ancient peoples was this regular cycle of sun–moon alignment. Twelve lunations (the period of one new moon to the next) of twenty-nine or thirty days gives a lunar calendar of 354 or 355 days, eleven days shorter than it takes the earth to orbit the sun. Pre-Islamic pilgrims would count twelve new moons from the 'head of the year' – *raas is-sana* – on the first day of the first month of the year (*al-muḥaram*) before arriving in Mecca for the three-day festival held in the final month of the lunar year – *dhu al-hijja* ('the month of the pilgrimage'). The names of Arabic months, some of which, like the third one, *rabi' al-a'wwal* ('the first spring'), referred to seasonal events, carried the same names both before and after the Age of Ignorance. Inter-tribal fighting was banned during four of them, including *al-muḥaram* (*ḥaram* – 'forbidden'). These forbidden months, the first, seventh (*rajab*), eleventh, and twelfth (*dhu al-qa'dah* and *dhu al-hijja*) were declared sacred by the Prophet and have remained so to this day.

A few years before Muhammed's flight to Medina, an entrepreneur, Qusai bin Quraysh, who controlled the pagan pilgrimage and its associated market fairs, worked out that if he inserted an additional month every three years, he could hold the date of the festival to the pleasant autumn months and thereby increase income for his tribe. This thirteenth month was abandoned by Muhammad, and since then the Muslim calendar has consisted of twelve months containing an alternating sequence of thirty and twenty-nine days. Additional days are intercalated to reconcile the date of the first day of the month with the date of the actual new moon. The ninth month of *ramadh'an* (which means 'scorching heat'), for example, moves backwards through the seasons and takes thirty-two and a half years to return to realignment with its starting point. As explained in Chapter 22, the Islamic calendar started from *al-hijra*, when the Prophet Muhammed emigrated to Medina in 622 CE. The lunar years from then carry the suffix 'AH' for 'after *al-hijra*' (not to be confused with *al-hijja*, the final month of the year).

For hubristic reasons best known to himself, President Gaddafi, whose squalid death in a conduit I did not regret, decided that the Libyan Islamic calendar should start either from the date of the Prophet's birth or his death, or both. One can imagine the confusion with a calendar which differed by up to fifty-two years from the standard. Fortunately most Islamic states use the Gregorian solar calendar for official business, reserving the Islamic lunar one for religious events. Arabic time can be equally confusing. It used to be the case that the Arabian time started from sunset rather than from midnight, as in the West. The hour of 'two o'clock' would therefore move relative to the fluctuating time of sunset, making bus and train times somewhat unpredictable. Again official business is now referred to standard time.

International Standard ISO 8601 states that Monday is the first day of the week. This is not so in Arabia, where the week starts on a Sunday. The word for 'day' is *youm*, so unsurprisingly the first day of the week is *al-youm al-ahad* ('the day the one') then 'the day the two' (Monday), etcetera, through to *al-yawm al-khamis* ('the day the five' – Thursday). Friday – *al-yawn al-jum'ah* – is the day of gathering for the noon prayer. The seventh and last day of the week, *al-yawm as-sabt* – our Saturday – comes from the verb 'to rest' or 'to sleep', similar to the Hebrew Sabbath and Greek sabaton, meaning 'to desist'; 'cease'; 'rest'.

In our still united but increasingly secular kingdom we 'celebrate' Easter and Christmas and enjoy an additional six national holidays fixed by act of Parliament. In Arabia, each state celebrates its own national day plus Islamic feasts of varying lengths depending on where they fall within the week. One-day holidays are celebrated at New Year (*waahid al-muharam*), the official birthday of the prophet (the twelfth day of *rabi al-a'wwal*), and the prophet's night journey and ascension (*lailat al-isra wa al-miraj*), which falls on the twenty-seventh day of the sacred month of *rajab*. The schism between the two main branches of Islam followed the battle of Karbala eighty kilometres southwest of Baghdad, which was fought on the tenth day of *al-muharam* in 680 CE and at which Husayn bin Ali, the grandson of the Prophet Muhamad, was killed. The Shi'a movement, which his death inspired, started in southern Iraq and was exported later into Persia by Arab colonists. This date is revered by the Shi'a, whose name comes from the Farsi *shiah-i-Ali* – 'Partisans of Ali'. The Sunni celebrate the same date as *ashura*, the day Noah left the ark and Moses later crossed the parted Red Sea, confounding Pharoah's chariots. The two most celebrated holidays – *eid* – from the Arabic verb *a'ouda* – 'to return' – are *eid al-fitr* (see below) and the longer *eid al-adha* – 'the feast of the sacrifice' – which are celebrated some forty days after *eid al-fitr*. The *eid* holiday starts on the tenth10th day of *dhu al hijja*, the last month of the Islamic year, when the *hajj* pilgrimage reaches its climax.

The start of the sacred month of Ramadhan is declared when the new moon is attested to have been seen by two qualified observers. It ends when the faintest crescent of the next new moon is sighted. This heralds the first day of the tenth month – *shawwal* – and the start of *eid al-fitr*, the festival of breaking the fast. This festival is a simply joyous family occasion, a time to renew ties with the extended family, call on one's shaykh to kiss his nose as a token of respect, and reaffirm the bond of tribal loyalty. I was caught up in such a celebration in a dusty seaside village at the foot of the Al Hajar mountains in Oman and made welcome with endless handshakes and sips of cardamon-flavoured coffee under a shady acacia tree, whose upper branches were filled incongruously with goats seeking the highest and tenderest shoots. Smiling youths discharged their rifles into the air. Children laughed and danced while donkeys with a rare day off brayed their approval. Just offshore on the silky azure sea (*azraq* – 'blue'), an anchored sharp-prowed *shu'i* fishing vessel nodded in unison as gentle waves slipped lazily up the shining beach, its sands as silvery as the new moon.

CHAPTER 27

و   waaw
واحد   waahid

One

In the early 1990s the only access to the spectacular 2,500-metre limestone plateau of Oman's *al-jebal al-akhdar* was via a narrow and rutted graded road winding up from the ruined village at the mouth of Wadi Ghul. The roofless light-brown walls of the houses, long abandoned by their residents, sheltered skinks and geckos and the occasional carpet viper warming itself on the hot rocks ready for the night hunt. Tourists were rare, but expatriates like me delighted in camping there overnight under a spectacular sky untouched by light pollution. Just beyond my favourite campsite, close to a gnarled acacia tree, black from not infrequent lightning strikes, lay a tiny hamlet.

This was home to two extended families of hardy mountain tribespeople overseen by a matriarch who eked out a basic living by selling goatshair rugs to the sporadic visitors. Her father, who looked eighty but was probably fifty, had an uncanny ability to know when we were coming. He would emerge from behind a rock with a few scraps of twisted wood to join us for coffee and a long-anticipated accompanying biscuit. Two bright and inquisitive eyes set above a thin grey beard and a mouth sporting a single tooth stared out of a face lined by hardship. His body, covered in a filthy grey dishdasha and a torn leather jacket, appeared to be made from dark brown whipcord, and he was very far from fragrant. But this was his home and we were grateful to share it with him. I would greet him with '*ahlan was sahlan, ya shaykh*'. Hands were shaken as he scanned our belongings with hawk-like intensity. We would then get down to business. 'Thank you for your gift of firewood. How much, O' shaykh?'

A thin, cunning smile would spread across his face as the index finger of his right hand rose upwards in an arc towards me. *'waahid rial,'* was the invariable response, the same price quoted if a guest wanted a photograph with him. He was therefore always known to my family as Al Waahid – 'The One'.

'Two' in Arabic is *'athneen,* and 'second' is *th'aniya* as in the fourth month of the Islamic calendar, *rabi ath-th'ani* ('the second spring'). Thani is a common name for a second son, the first (*al-awaal*) generally carrying the name of his grandfather. It does not convey any sense of being second best, although perhaps the author of *Spare* might disagree. One of the most impressive Arabs I had the honour to work with was called Thani. It was he who did so brilliantly on the long hydrographic course in the UK mentioned in Chapter 15. He later gained a Masters in the law of the sea from the University of Durham and became Oman's chief negotiator for maritime boundaries and subsequently, like me, its national Hydrographer. I tried to persuade him, with Sayyid Shihab's strong endorsement, to succeed me as the well-rewarded general manager of AMNAS, but he felt it his place to remain in the navy and finalise his boundary delimitation tasks. Honour and duty before all else. A very remarkable man and an example of all which is best in Arabia.

'Three' is *thal'atha.* It is an IALA convention that buoys marking a channel into a port are numbered consecutively from seaward, with green (starboard hand) buoys in Region A being painted with odd numbers. This is so that in reduced visibility the mariner can identify easily and unequivocally where his vessel is in the channel. The large 5-tonne channel marker number three on the approach to the port of Sohar was struck by a vessel under the command of an idiot when leaving the port at night. Next morning, our resident technician, who spoke almost no English but fluent grammar-less Arabic, rang me to report that *'al-thal'atha ma zain!'* And he was quite right – not good at all. The marker's cone-shaped top mark and self-contained marine lantern had been crushed. These were replaced within a few hours at a not inconsiderable cost, but who would pay? Little did the ship owner know that all our ports were covered by a vessel-tracking system known as AIS. The previous night's records for Sohar were checked and the culprit was quickly identified. My diligent administration manager summoned the shipping agent and after having been presented with the evidence, which the ship owner could not refute, the full cost of the repair was recovered which, unsurprisingly, at least to me, was fittingly three times the cost of the component parts.

'Four' is *arba'a*, 'fourteen' is *arba'ata'ashar*, and 'forty' is *arba'een*. A beautiful waterfall-filled *wadi* is named after the last of these and lies off the modern coastal road from Musqat to Sur. One still needs a 4WD vehicle to reach the villages, but when I last visited it, we walked. Hiking through the tall bird-filled reeds, wading through the streams, and swimming across the deep pools with ruined Portuguese watch towers above us was perfect. I asked the villagers of Mithqub why it was called *'arba'een*. No one knew for certain but claims of 'forty kilometres to its head' were obviously wrong, whereas 'forty families in the tribe' seemed possible. I will probably never know, but like so much in Oman, Wadi Arba'een was, and probably still is, magical.

The so-called 'Arabic' numerals, so common to us in the West, should more properly be called Western Arabic numerals to distinguish them from their Eastern Arabic cousins used in Arabia today. Both originated from third-century BCE Brahmi script, which split into western and eastern versions. The western version was used by Arabic-speaking scribes working in the Umayyad-ruled areas of the North African Maghreb region and Al-Andalus (Spain). Europeans gradually adopted the shape of these numerals from the tenth century CE onwards. They gained the soubriquet 'Arabic' as a result and had the advantage of being more cursive than the more rigorous linear Aramaic and Roman ones which they replaced. Those mathematically redundant Roman numerals survive today mostly in terms of showing date and time, the copyright year of Hollywood movies, dates of historic monuments, and on clocks, including the four recently refurbished faces of Parliament's Elizabeth Tower.

Eastern Arabic numerals, which Arabs refer to as *'farsi'* (i.e. Persian), are similarly modified versions of the earlier Indian script, with the numerals 7) ٧ ,(3) ٣ , (2) ٢ ,(1) ١), and 9) ٩) being similar to their western Arabic versions if one rotates ٣, ٢ and ٧ through 90°. This may be because scribes wrote on long parchments wrapped horizontally around their bodies, which were later rolled up into scrolls to be read vertically. Both numerical scripts, unlike Arabic itself, were designed to be written left to right, although a negative number is shown with the minus sign to the right of the numeral. For example, minus nine (-9) is written ٩ – . Unlike Roman numerals, a symbol for zero was included. This is a dot in the Eastern version called *sifr* in Arabic – the derivation of our word 'cipher'. Our symbol for zero (0) should not be confused with the similar Eastern Arabic symbol for 5 – *khamsa* (٥) – something which new arrivals in the Gulf often take time to absorb. The decimal point in Eastern Arabic is depicted as a comma (,). These numerals were used for mathematical and astronomical calculations in much of the Middle East until the twentieth century, while commerce was generally conducted using finger-counting methods.

Euclid, the Greek 'Father of Geometry', used graphical methods to solve, as Bertrand Russell put it, 'many things which we would naturally prove by algebra'. A little over a thousand years later, a remarkable academic and translator from a region of Greater Iran, Khwarazm, travelled to the Abbasid capital, Baghdad, in about 820 CE to work in the *bayt al-ḥikma* ('House of Wisdom'). His name was Abu Jafar Muhammad ibn Musa al-Khwarizmi, a prolific author and solver of linear and quadratic equations, who is rightly known as the 'Father of Algebra'. The word 'algebra' came from the title of his work, *The Compendious Book on Calculation by Completion and Balancing (al-kitab al-mukhtasar fi hisab al-jebr wa al-muqabala)*, *al-jebr* meaning 'completion' or resetting of anything broken. His ninth-century arithmetic treatise, *On the Calculation with Hindu Numerals*, was translated into Latin in the twelfth century as *Algoritimi de Numero Indorum*, which opens with 'Dixit Algorismi' – 'Thus spoke Al-Khwarizmi', the derivation of the word 'algorithm'.

Such was his legacy that the Latin translation of his hugely influential masterwork remained the major mathematical textbook in European universities until the sixteenth century. The fate of The House of Wisdom was less auspicious. It was sacked by Hulagu Khan's Mongol army in 1258 CE. Hulagu, like Kublai Khan, was a grandson of Genghis Khan, although the 'sacred' River Alph, which ran through Kublai's 'caverns measureless to man' in Coleridge's poem should not be confused with *'alf*, the Arabic for a thousand. The contents of the House of Wisdom's library were thrown into the River Tigris, their ink allegedly blackening the water. The leather covers of many irreplaceable works were ripped off to make sandals. A tragic example of ignorance personified.

CHAPTER 28

ي   yaa'
يسار   yas'ar

Left

Verbs in Arabic are generally listed in the third person singular form starting with 'ya', for example, *yatkalam* – 'he speaks'. However, other words beginning with the final letter of the Arabic alphabet, *yaa'*, are the second least common after those starting with that unusual-sounding letter *dhaa'* (Chapter 17). In the comprehensive Al-Mawrid Arabic-to-English dictionary, just 149 words and phrases which start with *yaa'* are shown, as opposed to words beginning with *meem* (Chapter 24), which are listed in their thousands. The first entry starting with yaa' is *ya'*, meaning 'O', as in '*ya' stef'n*' – 'O Stephen', or *ya' akhee* – 'O (my) friend'. This is the standard formal mode of spoken address throughout Arabia. The last word listed in that dictionary is *yoo yoo* – 'yo-yo'. How nice is that! Common nouns starting with yaa' are *yawm* ('day') and *yad* ('hand'). Hand gestures by Arabs very much form part of daily life, from the humble greeting with right hand on the breast or with the thumb and fingers pinched upwards together signifying that one should wait. A hand gesture never to get wrong is how to beckon someone towards you. This is done with the back of the right hand upwards and a slow curl of all fingers towards the palm. The western curled index finger with palm uppermost has a very different, and grossly insulting, meaning, so beware!

    The adjectives for 'left' and 'right' also start with *yaa'*. 'Left', *yas'ar*, is associated with ease and facility, to which we will return after considering the right. As mentioned in the first chapter, so much that one encounters in Arabia is related to what is good and fortunate on the right-hand side (*yameen*). These

191

can include customs. There is a fine tradition in Arabia where one honours another by manoeuvring oneself to be on the left when approaching a door or lift so that one can say, *'tafadhal – al yameen ya ustadh'* ('Please, go ahead, as you are on the right, O honoured one'). The other person, smiling broadly, may then take you by the hand and try to manoeuvre you to be on their right-hand side. This dance, full of protestations, may last for some time, but one's companion will eventually give way and accept (and remember) the proffered courtesy.

Yemen, that land of plenty which flourished from the frankincense trade, is now once again a very troubled country. External actors have been sponsoring rival factions to gain political control while its population, particularly children, suffer terrible hardship. I retain very fond memories of most of my visits there and interaction with its people. These have been recounted elsewhere in this book, but one visit was much less comfortable. This was an official trip to Aden a few months after the al-Qaeda suicide-boat attack on the *USS Cole* in October 2000 in which seventeen American sailors had been killed, many of them waiting in a lunch queue on the deck above the point of impact. Part of my remit as Royal Naval Liaison Officer (Gulf) based in the British Consulate in Dubai was to advise the commander-in-chief of where the diplomatic use of British warships might enhance the UK's reputation in the region. A reassuring ship visit to Aden after the *Cole* incident would, in my view, bolster Anglo–Yemeni relations and show that the Royal Navy was not cowed by threats from any terrorist organisation.

I had taken the previous commander-in-chief to tour the heavy-lift ship *MV Blue Marlin*, which was in Dubai en route to Aden to load the *Cole* for transport back to the US for repair. He had been promoted to First Sea Lord and shared his successor's view that a formal ship visit to Aden had value once a full risk assessment had been conducted. That was the reason for my trip, on which I was joined by the MI6 officer from our embassy in Sana'a and the very impressive naval attaché from Riyadh. Unlike the US agents who had been sent to investigate the bombing, we were all unarmed, with the two naval officers advertising our presence by wearing white tropical uniforms. If we were not targeted or harassed but welcomed warmly, then the risk to a visiting vessel would in all likelihood be less.

I joined some Yemeni soldiers in a watchtower overlooking the port. They were both astonished and delighted that I addressed them in their own tongue. They were confident of their own ability to guard the port and I felt that they were right. When I later returned to my hotel to change for the flight back to the UAE, I found the imprint of a hand on the back of my white uniform shirt, implanted by a smiling soldier who had been cleaning his rifle when I arrived. I found that rather reassuring. The Yemeni authorities were professional and our security was monitored discreetly, which was precisely the mood which we were keen to display to all observers, be they benevolent or otherwise. My commander-in-chief had told me in a telephone call before the visit that if I was happy for a visit to go ahead then he would be so too. The British trio agreed that all necessary risk-mitigation measures were effective, and *HMS Campbeltown* conducted an incident-free port call at Aden the following month.

I have lost touch with the young MI6 officer, but my naval attaché compatriot, Rupert, lives in an adjacent West Sussex village where he flourishes as an artist. After the tour of the port, we were keen to pay our respects to the military personnel who died during the Radfan Uprising culminating in the Battle of Crater in July 1967. They, with other casualties, lie in the low-walled rectangular compound of the Commonwealth War Graves Commission cemetery in *a'den as-sighirah* ('Little Aden'), watched over by a conscientious caretaker and towering jagged mountains. It is known as Silent Valley. Rupert and I stood there, heads bowed in the spring of 2001, and heard just the wind, which raised little jinns of dusty sand amid the perfectly maintained paths.

Yasser (or Yasir) is a common name in Arabia. Many are named after 'Ama'r ibn Yasir, one of the Prophet Muhammad's closest friends and allies, who is revered by all Muslims. The name was adopted in the early 1950s by a person whose full name was Mohammed Abdel Rahman Abdel Raouf Arafat al-Qudwa al-Husseini, that less-than-easy character, Yasser Arafat. His complicated relationship with the West and both Arab and Israeli leaders frustrated a lasting solution to the foundation of a Palestinian state. A few years before Arafat adopted his name, and in the year which I was born, another and very different personality, Shaykh Yasir al-Junuba, reluctantly helped Wilfred Thesiger to cross Oman. His route from the edge of the Wahiba Sands to the border of Abu Dhabi ran through the hostile (to Christians) heartland of Oman, governed in those days by the *imam* based in Nizwa, not the Sultan in Musqat. When the *imam* eventually granted Thesiger safe passage, he travelled with the imam's representative and a shaykh from the al-Duru tribe, a man who, so Thesiger reported, 'possessed the charm which Yasir so sadly lacked'.

A much more charming Arab bearing that name was my technical manager in AMNAS, Yasser al-Yahmadi. He never stopped smiling and embodied every aspect of ease and facility, as well as the ability to make things possible, exactly as the meaning of his name implied. Yasser accompanied me to the IALA international conference held in Shanghai in 2006 and charmed everyone he met from all the nations represented, some of whom had had a previously ill-informed opinion of Arabs. He was particularly impressive when attending the final conference dinner held in the rotating restaurant at the top of the Shanghai Tower, 600 metres above the River Huangpu. Yasser appeared dressed in a spotless white dishdasha and thobe, a *massar* on his head and a curved silver khunjar inserted into the embroidered cloth wrapped around his waist. Quite how he got that dagger through Chinese customs I shall never know. Easy charm, probably.

My twenty-eight chapters are almost complete. What is left to say? I spent almost twenty years of my life living in Arabia and met my wonderful wife there. Our house carries reminders of those years in the form of pictures, carpets, and artefacts, some of which I brought, others given to me as gifts. The one-metre tall engraved silver-plated coffee pot and stand presented to me by the officers of the Royal Navy of Oman hydrographic service would not look out of place in the centre of an Arabic roundabout. His Highness Shihab bin Tariq's parting gift of a silver ship on a golden sea, in which 'float' three gold-and-silver inlaid Venetian glass-stoppered perfume bottles, is bling personified. I have been incredibly fortunate, *il-humdu-allah*. I shared four of those Arabian years with my twin brother, Andy, who you may recall from the opening chapter tried to drag me into the Red Sea. After we were evacuated from Jordan in the mid-fifties we lived in West Cornwall and shared such adventures. Sadly, he died from a brain tumour just before he reached his sixtieth birthday. I scattered his ashes on Trencrom Hill, which overlooks St Ives Bay to the north and St Michael's Mount to the south. I hope to join him there one day to see out what might be left of eternity, but my heart will remain in Arabia.

ACKNOWLEDGEMENTS

As any new author comes to realise, the inspiration for writing a specific work comes from within but needs encouragement and fertilisation from external sources. I tilled the creative ground of my imagination when I retired from the Royal Navy just over twenty years ago and started research on a potential 'biography' of Arabia. A very helpful and renowned literary agent, Toby Eady (died 2017), was kind enough to propose that I took a different tack. In this he was supported, as in all aspects of my life, by my wife, Annie, to whom this book is dedicated. However, my return to Oman and subsequent other career moves delayed real progress on this manuscript. A combination of Covid and a letter from HMRC demanding advance payment for the next financial year convinced me to retire, and with more time available, my 2023 New Year's resolution was to follow Toby Eady's advice. This I have done, and my thanks go to him somewhat belatedly.

I have been very fortunate to have been encouraged and challenged throughout my working life by some great people. I acknowledge first and foremost my mentor, Captain Richard Campbell OBE Royal Navy (died 2023), without whose inspirational leadership I would have gone well astray. The second person to whom I owe a debt of thanks is His Highness Shihab bin Tariq Al Said, who was my boss in Oman both in their navy and as chairman of the commercial company I worked for subsequently. I also acknowledge the guidance and encouragement of Rear Admiral Jean-Charles LeClair, who recruited me to join him in the newly established IALA World-Wide Academy, where

I became its vice dean. Without his foresight, I would not have travelled so extensively in the South Pacific nor become a visiting professor of the Navigation Institute of Jimei University, Xiamen!

While writing this book, I read two particularly brilliant works. The first, *Black Wave*, by Kim Ghattas, covered the rivalry between Saudi Arabia and Iran and touched on many aspects of the ongoing conflict in the Middle East region. Ms Ghattas covered different ground than I have done, but her insight was inspirational. The second book was *Colonialism* by Professor Nigel Biggar, whose fact-based arguments focused my mind considerably. I wish to thank them both.

I am grateful to a number of my friends and family who provided honest feedback on the initial drafts of certain chapters. In particular, I send my loving thanks to both of my sons, Luke and Daniel Bennett, and to my elder grandson, Youcef Azzaz. Adrian Drummond, Francesca Pradelli, Miranda Shonia, Graham Stoddart-Stones and Gerardine Delanoye are all stars in their own right.

Penultimately I acknowledge the support of the team at Novum Publishing, without whom this manuscript would have just gathered dust.

But finally, I wish once again to acknowledge the clear-sighted, no-nonsense, critical skills of my wife, Annie, who painstakingly proof-read each chapter and provided precisely the right level of advice, including her proposal for its title, which of course was pitch-perfect. This book would not have reached its conclusion without her. How lucky am I?

BIBLIOGRAPHY

The following books and documents were consulted when writing this book:
Dr Rohi Baalbaki. *Al-Mawrid – A Modern Arabic-English Dictionary.* (Dar EL-ELM LILMALAYIN 2001)
James Lunt. *Glubb Pasha.* (Harvill Press 1984)
John Bagot Glubb. *The Great Arab Conquests.* (Quartet Books 1980)
T. E. Lawrence. *Seven Pillars of Wisdom.* (Penguin Books 1962)
Michael Asher. *Lawrence – The Uncrowned King of Arabia.* (Penguin Books 1998)
C. M. Doughty. *Passages from Arabia Deserta.* (Penguin Books 1983)
Wilfred Thesiger. *Arabian Sands.* (HarperCollins 1990)
Stafford Bettesworth Haines. *Memoir of the S. and E. Coasts of Arabia.* (The Journal of the Royal Geographical Society of London, Vol. 15 1845)
Richard Burton. *The First Voyage of Sindbad the Seaman (from The Thousand Nights and One Night).* (Casanova Society 1923)
Freya Stark. *The Southern Gates of Arabia.* (Arrow Books 1990)
Petroleum Development Oman LLC. *Oman's Geographical Heritage.* (PDO 2006)
Manie Grobler. *A Field Guide to the Larger Mammals of Oman.* (The Ministry of Regional Municipalities, Environment & Water Resources, Sultanate of Oman – date not shown)
Michael McKinnon. *Arabia – Sand. Sea. Sky.* (BBC Books 1990)
Paul Johnson. *Civilizations of the Holy Land.* (Weidenfeld and Nicolson 1979)
J. G. Lorimer. *Gazetteer of the Persian Gulf, Oman and Central Arabia Vol.1.* (Superintendent Government Printing, India 1915)

Sultan Muhammad Al-Qasimi. *The Gulf in Historic Maps 1478 – 1861*. (Privately published 1999)

Sultan Muhammad Al-Qasimi. *The Myth of Arab Piracy in The Gulf*. (Croom Helm 1986)

Bertrand Russel. *History of Western Philosophy*. (George Allen & Unwin 1991)

Unknown. *The Expeditions Against The Bani Bu Ali*. (Typewritten document, date unknown)

The Koran. (Penguin Classics 1990)

Oman – a seafaring nation. (Ministry of National Heritage and Culture, Sultanate of Oman 1991)

S. B. Miles. *The Countries and Tribes of the Persian Gulf*. (Frank Cass & Co. Ltd 1966)

Richard Trench. *Arabian Travellers*. (Macmillan London 1986)

André Stevens. *Citadels Between Sand and Sea*. (Terra Incognita Publishing House, Belgium 1990)

Maxime McKendry. *Seven Hundred Years of English Cooking*. (Treasure Press 1973)

Nigel Biggar. *Colonialism*. (William Collins 2023)

Hugh Thomas. *The Slave Trade – The History of the Atlantic Slave Trade 1440 – 1870*. (Phoenix Paperback 2006)

Albert Hourani. *A History of the Arab Peoples*. (Faber & Faber 1991)

Bernard Lewis. *The Middle East*. (Phoenix Giant Paperback 1996)

Oman. (Department of Information – Muscat 1972)

Karen Armstrong. *A History of God*. (William Heinemann 1993)

Alfred Guillaume. *Islam*. (Penguin Books 1956)

Akbar S. Ahmed. *Discovering Islam*. (Routledge & Kegan Paul 1990)

The author

After a childhood spent in Egypt and Jordan, Stephen joined the Royal Navy and specialised as a hydrographic surveyor. He served in Antarctica, the Middle East, and the Far East, the Caribbean and European waters. He saw action in two wars and commanded two ships and a specialist naval school before retiring after thirty-five years' service, the last ten of which were based in Arabia.

Stephen subsequently returned to Oman for six years to manage a private company for a member of the Omani royal family before joining a Paris-based international organisation concerned with standards for the safety of marine navigation, towards the end of which he was appointed as visiting professor to the Navigation Institute of Jimei University, Xiamen, China. Stephen now lives in West Sussex, where he is a school governor and chair of a local charity.

novum PUBLISHER FOR NEW AUTHORS

The publisher

*He who stops
getting better
stops being good.*

This is the motto of novum publishing, and our focus is on finding new manuscripts, publishing them and offering long-term support to the authors.
Our publishing house was founded in 1997, and since then it has become THE expert for new authors and has won numerous awards.

Our editorial team will peruse each manuscript within a few weeks free of charge and without obligation.

You will find more information about
novum publishing and our books on the internet:

www.novum-publishing.co.uk

Printed in Great Britain
by Amazon